To Joy,

May the blessings of
love and beauty be
with you always on
your sacred journey.

Nancy
5/6/17

Praise for *A Magdalene Awakens...*

A Magdalene Awakens, Hidden Temple Secrets, guides you into a fascinating journey of ancient secrets whose time is now, to be remembered and known. Nancy Safford's skills and gifts as a clairvoyant, shaman, and Priestess of the Temple of Isis and the Magdalene Mysteries reveals these secrets of a very ancient sisterhood of Priestess "Keepers" whose work and mission is illuminated in this visionary story of planetary service. Ages past, and current time are interwoven, as the pieces of this sacred story are gathered, assembled, and revealed. - J. Maloney, Author and Professor, Sedona, AZ

Nancy Safford is taking us on a remarkable outer and inner journey from Arizona, to England and Southern France where she finds herself bringing ancient knowledge back to present day... This is a page-turner and I promise that you will be right there with her on her amazing spiritual road of discovery. - A. Spuhler, Vortex Guide and Wellness Coach, Sedona, AZ

Nancy Safford is a spiritual adventurer who you will want to travel with. Her beautifully told story, in which she, through her growing spiritual insight and intuition, takes you with her to discover sacred mysteries relating to Mary Magdalene, the Divine Feminine and more. - C. Newton, screenplay writer, Tucson, AZ

Nancy is a gifted writer. Her story carried me to places where I met beings and spirits unknown to me. I felt her beside me as we journeyed gracefully into new worlds and ancient temples, where she brought them to life. This was Nancy's gift to me. It is her gift to the world. - P. Thomas, poet, writer and artist, Charlottesville, VA.

Dedication

To all women and men on a Journey
To Remember
I dedicate this book to you.

Always follow your Dreams
And allow them to bring you
Home...To Yourself

A Magdalene Awakens

Hidden Temple Secrets

Nancy Safford

First Printing

ISBN-13: 978-1543240986
ISBN-10: 1543240984

Introduction

When I discovered ancient secrets hidden in a temple in southern France, it seemed essential that I reveal the story of what led me to find them. A long guarded secret, it is part of the Rennes Le Chateau mystery in the Languedoc area of southern France, which carries a legacy that was possibly left there by early masters and alchemists, and guarded by Priestesses who knew the workings of this inner temple.

My story begins more than twenty years ago, when my life became an amazing adventure as soon as I moved to Sedona, Arizona in the southwestern part of the United States. Having an earlier career in photography, I begin my story with photographs because I had no words for what I carried deep inside. I didn't know the story that wanted to be told. It took years before I wanted more understanding of the faces and mysterious things that began appearing in my photographs.

One day they began revealing themselves to me, physically, so I could communicate with them. Soon I realized they were calling me to see, know and understand that there was something else available in this world. Thus my story was written so I could understand what this part of my life has been about, but ultimately it is a story for all people to realize that there are many possibilities and choices that can be made on one's life journey.

A larger calling than I could have ever imagined when Sedona called me, little did I know the journey would be so full of magic and mystery, that it would re-direct my life. One moment I am innocently sitting by the peaceful creek waters of Sedona, the next I am leading groups to southern France and hearing messages from beings deep within some ancient temple there.

"What is happening to me," I would have asked if I'd seen at the beginning how my life would evolve: a new marriage, becoming a shamanic practitioner, a Priestess and even a spiritual guide for others, first in Sedona, then in France. This book shows how I became more familiar with the inner and outer worlds, with nature and its mysteries and how I gained knowledge, but also experienced great vulnerability. I learned that I had attachments as soon as I surrendered to the unknown.

From those first spirit faces in my photographs asking for my recognition, to elusive figures spinning in the waters before me, or speaking to me from the rocks and trees, I had unmistakably stepped through some doorway into another place, veiled from this physical reality.

I would never have known that my journey to Sedona would be the beginning to something so elusively spectacular. Meeting animal allies gave me strength, support, when soon I was fearlessly exploring whatever mystery pulled me. Ever unfolding there seemed to be no end to what I could discover, I learned, like all cycles that are eternal. At what point we step into it however, is our choice.

First hoping to understand the photos that called me into these other worlds, I later realized this calling was actually to a place deep within myself, to my own magic. Furthermore everything in my story actually happened to me, no matter what reality it might have been. These experiences became my truth that I now share with you.

I have also written this story because I retrieved wisdom from deep within the Earth, from the great mother. It is an ancient code that not only lives in special places hidden in the Earth, but it is deep within our hearts, a Divine Design that has been with us since the beginning. I discovered mine in France and learned that now it is time to wake it up, to remember who I am, have been and always will be. This is also an invitation for each of you.

My soul is now more peaceful. My feminine self, my Priestess self, feels alive, honored, after finally being resurrected and reclaimed, ready to walk the ancient timelines of eternity once again. I am not alone because you are with me; we are in this together. This book, my story, will validate that it is so. A wondrous journey it has been.

Contents

Chapter One – A Diamond Vehicle

Slowly, very slowly, it glided into view. Suspended in the open space outside my balcony window, it floated there. It was nearly twenty feet high.

No.....No! I heard myself suddenly cry out from a voice deep inside, as if something were coming to get me. I was alone in the apartment, my partner gone for several days.

"It's a moving Diamond. No….it's a moving Diamond Pyramid," I exclaimed out loud as if there was someone standing next to me. A *vehicle* it was unlike anything I'd ever seen.

Just an hour earlier writhing with sudden pain in my stomach I'd climbed the stairs as fast as possible to my bedroom to lie down. My friend's anger had affected me as soon as I shut the door behind her. Destitute, her husband had left her.

Ever since my move to Sedona and its spinning vortices six months earlier, they had opened my fields so wide I had no defenses. It seemed like I was taking on other people's negative energies.

As soon as my pain lessened I sat up, my back against the headboard to look outside the balcony window as the light softened in its approach toward evening. I liked to admire the beautiful red rocks in the distance and watch anything flying by. Sometimes it was an occasional red tailed hawk searching for its dinner, which too often became a small bird eating the seeds we'd left them under the trees below.

Gathering courage, I bent forward as this mysterious vehicle hovered before me. I wanted to look at it straight on. *It was almost transparent!*

Quickly, my eyes went inside and settled on an elderly grey bearded man dressed in a white hooded robe. He was looking back at me. *Zap!* Something hit me. Not outside, inside, within me. All the pain left in my throbbing stomach was gone. Completely dissolved. I pinched myself to see if I was awake and in my body or if this experience was coming from a dream. Nope, I was definitely here.

Longing to identify the being, I asked myself: *Was the being some kind of angel like Gabriel or maybe even Raphael?*

I observed the diamond vehicle more closely noticing how the figure fit comfortably inside with no room for anyone else. I couldn't help wondering, if it was his personal traveling vehicle. But the longer we continued glancing at each other, back and forth, it seemed like one moment his presence was of formless light next to me in my room, the next, he was back in his *diamond vehicle* watching me. Sometimes it was as if his eyes were only of light, the next, they were transformed into a hazel-like color.

With no recollection of how much time had passed, I was getting comfortable. My spirit felt elated, calm, with a sense of inner joy I couldn't remember feeling before. Was this unique encounter with a being from *another world* in a timeless moment a regular occurrence in Sedona or was it something else? Certainly it had engaged me so completely, as if there was no end to it. I was blind to other details around me.

But then suddenly, like a flash of lightning the vehicle whooshed itself away and disappeared as mysteriously as it had appeared.

Please No! I said, *No*, as tears began streaming from my eyes. My back still against the bed's headboard, but with the fastest move I'd made all day, I pushed back the covers and catapulted myself across the room to open the sliding glass door of the balcony. Stepping over to the railing to look out, I stretched my neck in every possible direction searching for any rock formation behind which it could have hidden. Desperate.

Where could it have disappeared so fast, I asked, watching the sky carefully, while perching myself on the edge of the cold plastic balcony chair. I gazed out at the horizon, searching for any tiny movement in the distance. There was nothing.

As if something inside me had collapsed my heart felt empty. The diamond vehicle and the elusive angel-like being inside were gone. Calming myself, I questioned: *Was someone trying to contact me from another timeline? Was I supposed to remember something?*

Chapter 2 – My Journey West

Winds pushed against my face, sometimes softly, sometimes not, as I went back and forth from my second floor apartment to my car, loading suitcases and everything necessary for a two month journey. It was mid June 1992 as I left the Adirondack Mountains of upstate New York on my first cross-country trip, alone, to the southwest, Sedona, in Arizona.

Excited to leave the northeast for a new adventure, I sensed something was changing in my life. My first day of driving, I began to reflect on it. Spontaneously, thoughts came up about my work as a photographer, twenty-five years now, whereby I was always capturing light, how it played on people's faces or bodies and how it dramatized extraordinary scenes in nature. My photographs were always showing others what I saw, what touched me in the outer world. Now however, it was time to learn more about those worlds recorded in the mysterious photos from the exhibit I just took down, titled, *Shots From The Unknown*.

These photographs had recorded something else, maybe from another reality or world about which I had no answers. When people asked me, "How did this one happen," pointing to a specific photograph hanging on the wall, or asking, "How did you know this was there" or "What did you do to make that appear," I couldn't respond because I didn't know. What I did know was that I always photographed alone in order to experience my feelings in each moment, what was around me so I could record it in my camera.

Interestingly, in each of these photographs I recorded a face of some kind of a *being* or person I never saw when taking the picture. Many of these images happened during my two years living in France, while documenting the last of the French peasant farmers, traditionally farming with oxen and using the old threshing machines.

All black and white images, one photo was of a tall figure wearing a white robe standing under a group of trees next to a sheep pasture, while in another I captured a large face on the wall of a small 16th century chapel that showed big eyes watching the same baptism I was attending. A peasant family was having their newborn child baptized. Another was taken on Martha's Vineyard Island, when a large face was looking out at me from the middle of a pond one misty spring morning.

Thus I drove the long route west, with these images in my psyche, hoping to learn more about these unknown worlds that a part of me seemed to be accessing. The question was: *What part of me was responding to them? Was it my subconscious mind, my unconscious self or something else*?

Furthermore, it was time to address my early childhood visions of moving things, possibly spirits, inside the historic house where we lived until I was seven. They scared me; no one could explain what they were so I tried to shut them off. It worked but I was still scared of the dark until I was in my mid twenties. Now the time had come to know more about this other reality, this *otherworld*. I asked myself: *What would I have to do to see it? Would it be scary*? But more importantly: *Was I ready?*

By understanding these elusive worlds, maybe I could learn about the bigger picture of my life. In fact, my journey to the southwest had been initiated by a small voice deep inside calling me to Sedona, to possibly move there.

Then suddenly while driving along, it began to feel like I was following some kind of diagonal line pulling me from the northeast to the southwest, as if my car was on some kind of "track" and something else was driving, until, after four long days, it stopped. I was at the foot of the famed Sangre de Cristo Mountains that surrounded the oldest city in the country, Santa Fe, New Mexico.

After navigating my way into town, I noticed light colored mud and straw built adobe dwellings on each side of the road, before I arrived in the square, the central plaza area. It felt peaceful as I parked my car. Then I noticed a small outside café in one corner of this plaza, so I walked over and sat down, ready to order something.

Santa Fe could easily have been my choice to stay for these next two months, exploring the magic of this seemingly timeless city. It was known to be the oldest in the country and probably carried great wisdom from its earlier Native Americans, the Pueblo people. But I had chosen Sedona, where I had already been several times.

However, my reason for stopping here now was because I had an invitation to introduce "holography" to a group of young 6th grade Native Americans in the public Indian School here. They wanted me to teach them how to make a 3-D image, a hologram.

A Native American physicist who worked at Los Alamos National Laboratory had recommended me to the school after I'd met him a year earlier. I was visiting Santa Fe with a friend who knew him. We discussed my work in upstate New York, where I had successfully pioneered bringing holography into education in an interdisciplinary approach. He was noticeably impressed.

Working in holography was also about working with light. It was about the organization of light inside a laser that allowed a three dimensional image to be captured on a flat holographic film plate. It was a Nobel Prize winning physics concept.

Working with children from the third grade level up to the twelfth grade, I had simplified it for each to understand. In fact I thought I could write a book about the different ways children learned, from those I worked with over the years, gifted and highly gifted, to children "at risk", "special needs" or even dyslexic children. Now I was about to have an entirely new experience working with young Native American students.

Just two days later, as I set up equipment on the steel top table Los Alamos Lab had constructed for me to stabilize the laser light from the minutest vibration, we were ready.

With my lens placed in front of the laser beam, to expand it, thousands of light particles were then suspended next to each other, seeming to move in space. Mesmerized, I watched as two young Indian boys, each with their long black hair and dark eyes enticed each other to try and capture one of these light particles on their finger.

Standing next to each other, one said to the other, "Hey, try this, I can feel this particle on my finger." So the other boy, a little shorter and rounder in the stomach, put his finger in the floating tiny particles of the red light and replied, "Yup, I feel the energy; maybe this particle will come away with me," as I watched him try to divert one or two of the seemingly dancing light particles away, outside of the beam.

He seemed to think it was like a tiny fly that he could take away with him. But having no luck, he asked his friend, "Why won't it go, what keeps it here?"

With no answer from his friend, he was quiet for a moment. Then he asked, "Do you think this tiny particle is carrying an ancient message from a far away place in the universe? Maybe it can teach us something."

Again his friend didn't respond, as he was seemingly lost in his own world, moving his finger back and forth into the expanded laser beam, leaving the shorter boy to find his own answer.

Astonished by their questions to each other, the likes I'd never heard from any students previously, I had no significant answers for them either.

Months later however, I learned that Native Americans have always lived with the knowledge that everything has consciousness, from rocks and trees to water and the tiniest of stones. Thus, why wouldn't a light particle be carrying a message too?

I complimented them on how perceptive they were and explained what happens inside the laser tube as an atom changes from a sleeping state into an excited state, as the two gases, helium and neon (in this laser) travel back and forth between the two inside mirrors, one at each end of the laser, to elevate their state. Then one gas absorbs the other and emits a "photon". These "excited photons" are what comes out of a laser tube.

Each child then found an object to fit in the 4x5 inch size of the film, something that reflected light, as a white shell would. In this "single beam reflection hologram," the exposure lasted for sixty seconds before it was developed in a tray, similar to the early days of photography.

After drying the film, we could view the object projecting out in front of the film or behind it - dimensionally. If the right light source wasn't available to see it, then nothing was visible on the film. Thus these six graders thought it was like creating *magic.*

They kept asking me how something could be there one minute – with a light - and then gone the next, without a light? It was not at all like a photograph. They understood that the image was there regardless, but were mesmerized by something appearing and then disappearing, like it was some kind of *illusion* or *vision.* They carried this question with them after the program was over.

I was very excited, because it was one of my original reasons for teaching holography, so children could truly understand about illusion, what you can see sometimes, while at other times you see nothing. But it is always there.

Perhaps I had more to contemplate then they did when we were done. Their questions of "consciousness" and the light particles had not entered my vocabulary as often as it had theirs, I realized. They had been born into certain traditional knowledge, wisdom, passed down since long before they were born.

Moreover, the program was highly successful and I was invited to come back to the San Felipe Pueblo, one of the nearby pueblos, to do a similar program. I accepted.

After a day of rest, it was time to continue my journey to Sedona. As I drove out of Santa Fe I realized that my world was about to change, my understanding of life and myself in it. Of the many roads I could have chosen, I had chosen this one.

Chapter 3 – Sedona

The road west from New Mexico to Arizona was so straight it seemed not a curve was in it. I passed through several Indian Reservations: the Acoma Pueblo, the Zuni Reservation and then the Navajo Reservation. But after crossing the Arizona border, I was still on the Navajo Reservation and recognized that it extended into both states.

Feeling like I was heading west into oblivion, I was like Dorothy on her journey into OZ where nothing was known for sure. I could have gone 100 miles per hour or even 200 mile per hour easily because the land was so flat. However no matter how fast I drove, I couldn't escape questions coming up about the new choices in my life.

After my experience with these exceptionally perceptive Native American children, I wondered why I had decided to stop doing holography in the schools? I asked myself why I wanted to move to Arizona and leave New York State? Being motivated to offer holography in the schools for so long was also in response to a small voice in my head telling me to do it. Thus it felt as if I had been on a "mission."

Happy that so many schools now worked with holography across upstate New York, I could now comfortably let it go. I was ready for a new adventure with no clue as to what it was. Indeed I was taking a blind step into the *unknown*.

It was late on that hot July afternoon, when I arrived in Flagstaff. Turning off the highway, I drove down the winding descent through Oak Creek Canyon to Sedona. A rim of high limestone and sandstone cliffs, tinted red and white, were on both sides of me now as I navigated my car around the twisting and turning 2,500 foot drop, carved out from thousands of years of evolution. It felt like I was going through a birthing canal between the closeness of these canyon walls, pushing me out of the womb into uptown Sedona.

Feeling birthed, I felt the magnetism of the red rocks. Each was a different shape and height from the one beside it; they were calling me closer. I wanted to pull my car over and gaze at them, but would do that another day. I had been to Sedona twice before, first hearing about it from a friend. She not only talked about the vortex energies, but the endless red rock formations within them.

Following directions to my rental house in the west part of Sedona, I turned right onto a narrow road and continued straight to its end. I found the house and parked my car as a deep sigh of relief came over my body. My brain had a moment of no thoughts, leaving me frozen there for a minute in the void. I had arrived.

Reaching for my suitcase and the small grocery bag of items I'd just bought, I climbed the stairs to the house and walked over to the front door. I grasped for the handle when I saw a praying mantis perched on the screen. With its head slightly lifted, it seemed to be greeting me. I noticed its transparent belly was larger than any I'd seen before and quickly thought, *Maybe it's pregnant.* It remained perched there while I carefully opened the door.

Once inside, instead of stepping down to test the couch or choose one of the two bedrooms, I dropped my suitcase, placed the grocery bag on the kitchen counter and followed my curiosity onto the back patio under the shade of the trees.

Selecting a pale green patio chair I slid into it and surrendered willingly relieved that it supported my back so well. Minutes passed before I decided to return to the kitchen and brew a cup of tea.

Walking under the arched doorway to the kitchen, I opened a cupboard door, selected a cup with a cactus design, discovered the teapot below and heated some water. In a short time, tea in hand, I was back out to the patio with the view of Thunder Mountain. It was the high butte behind my new house in the middle of West Sedona.

Time disappeared, when soon I began asking myself what else would I do in this enchanted land for two months? My journey here had been inspired by a tiny voice inside that told me to move here and to possibly leave everything I'd accomplished behind.

Still lost in my thoughts, I walked back into the house and chose one of the two bedrooms. It was the one with the nice queen sized bed with two windows, one looking out toward Thunder Mountain behind the house, the other looking out the front toward the high mesa table-like shape in the middle of west Sedona, Airport Mesa.

Lastly, I opened my suitcase, hung a few dresses and shirts in the closet, found the case with my toiletries in it, and went into the bathroom to run a bath. Already early evening, it was time to nurture myself.

Undressing, I climbed into the hot waters and took a big breath. I was tired. Sliding the body butter soap over my arms, legs and face felt nurturing. It brought me back into the present moment, before I was ready to step out and put on fresh clothes. I made a simple salad for dinner and ate it on the back terrace. I was comfortable here and I slept well this first night.

Inspired that next morning, I drove the windy road down to sit beside the creek at Red Rock Crossing,

Cathedral Rock, by the soothing waters. It was a place I'd discovered and loved on previous visits to Sedona. Feeling welcomed, I sat with my hot feet dangling in the water, looking up at the two tall spires in the distance.

A day later I called Lynne, the only person I knew in Sedona to say hello. She'd moved here months previously and was the one who originally told me about Sedona. Also from upstate New York, she led meditations and facilitated other kinds of healings for people, so after attending several of her meditations we became friends.

Since she knew Sedona better then me, I asked if she had any suggestions of something fun to do. Without hesitation she recommended a jeep ride, telling me which jeep company and which tour to ask for, so I did.

The morning of the tour, just stepping into the jeep was already a new adventure. After the driver gathered our small group we drove to an isolated area, where we all got out. Down a remote path we moved over to a ridge of flat red rocks, whereby he presented us with an unusual exercise. "Move in every possible way so you can shake loose, then release all the old things you might be carrying, inside, outside, that are no longer important in your lives". He started shaking his body around to demonstrate how he suggested we move our bodies.

I had never done anything like this. And the exercise was magnified when I looked out at the others shaking around and moving on the rocks, up and down, twisting and turning in such unimaginable ways. I soon admitted actually liking doing this; it was very different than anything I'd experienced before and I felt lighter after, as though something might easily have been released. It was easy to admit that I wouldn't find people moving like this in upstate New York.

After spending lots of time on the hidden pathways around the red rocks and in the deep canyons, and after being touched by the many ancient faces I found hidden on the rocks and the wild coyotes walking freely on the paths, I called to ask my friend, again, for more suggestions of what to do.

I was sitting on my patio in my favorite chair when she, in response made a long sigh. I heard her take a breath in and then let it out before she said, "Nothing, do nothing."

Dumbfounded, my memory quickly flashed back to my stepmother, who was often exhausted by my abundance of energy as a child, telling me to slow down and to stop going so fast. I always had so many ideas of things to do.

I tried to imagine what it would be like to stop moving so fast. Being such a curious child, it was hard then, but now, I was being challenged again by the possibility of actually slowing down.

The praying mantis was still on the screen, though it had moved to the back patio door, perhaps wanting to keep me company. I couldn't understand how it could stay in the same position for so long, doing what seemed to be, nothing. I never saw it move and soon wondered if it had something to teach me.

Chapter 4 – The Meeting

The phone rang a day later. It was Lynne. She realized there was something she could recommend, to have a session with a highly respected "channel" she liked, so I got his number and made an appointment for the following day.

It was late morning when my car crossed the small bridge over the creek waters. Following my directions I turned left, then right, noticing the different colored trailers of pale pink, white and various shades of tan. Some had tall plants growing in front, others brightly colored pots of red geraniums or yellow sunflowers.

I parked my car under a tree and got out to search for Robert's trailer. After walking around a few of these other trailers, I spotted a small silver trailer tucked in behind an old white one with a pink geranium in front. Anticipating my arrival Robert had stepped outside the door so I walked over to introduce myself to him.

Very tall with slightly stooped shoulders and grey peppered hair that reached his shoulders, he greeted me with a gentle smile and invited me inside. His turquoise and white stripped western shirt, cowboy boots and jeans were a norm for me after recently spending a year photographing bull riding and bronco-riding cowboys for my first photo story for *Adirondack Life Magazine*.

As I entered his small trailer I could see that everything was neatly in place. One chair had a tall back with well-worn armrests and a comfortably worn seat. I knew it was his favorite as he lowered himself into it. I was invited to sit in the chair opposite.

Lynne told me that Robert allowed several different beings to speak through him, offering insights for people such as myself searching for answers. From an earlier teacher I'd had in New York who did trance channeling, I was aware of the procedure. A person goes into a trance or leaves his or her body allowing a spirit-person to borrow it who then talks through him or her. A person's voice can change completely.

Thus I watched as Robert moved into his position, angled a little to the right side of his chair, with both feet firmly on the floor, the toes of his boots pointing out from under his jeans. His face began to change. With his eyes closed tight his mouth began to curve up at the edges; he was bringing in the spirit guide who wanted to speak to me.

"This is Speaks of Many Truths," the being said who went on to identify himself as a Native American Elder. "And I am here to talk to you today. I see you have come to Sedona because there is much you wish to learn here."

As he spoke, Robert's voice continued in a flowing rhythm that had a high intonation of words and then slipped down into a lower tone, like a wave that went up and then came down. He spoke a lot to me, but I remembered most his last words, "And you will need to slow down your pace, not to miss what nature is going to reveal to you," before he finished with, "Nature is alive and can speak to you if you are ready to listen." Then he was quiet for a few minutes as Speaks of Many Truths left and Robert returned to his body, ready to speak as himself again.

I found it a paradox how Robert's presence was of a tall stately being that one might think would command a loud voice and sweeping movements, but no. His words were gentle and his movements smooth and subtle. In fact, I found that he already had a calming effect on me.

He reached for the glass of water he'd left on the table by his chair before the session, lifted it and drank. Then I thanked him for the session and related how there were some new insights I would be working with. I mentioned that from my career as a photographer how I loved to photograph the beauty of nature and its patterns, but what Speaks of Many Truths was referring to about the consciousness of nature was indeed a different perspective. Thus I would wait for nature to "speak" to me.

I opened my purse and found the money for my session and handed it to him. A minute of silence lapsed between us before I got up to leave. Quickly, Robert mentioned that he had to go to Flagstaff in the afternoon for a chiropractic appointment and matter-of-factly said, "Would you like to drive up with me, we could have lunch after?" I answered, "Yes, that would be nice," not having any idea why he invited me.

His cranberry colored Toyota sedan moved easily around the bends in the winding canyon road, as we climbed the 2500 feet up to Flagstaff, back up the birthing canal I had descended through days earlier when I arrived in Sedona.

I sat in the waiting room during his appointment, after which we drove to his favorite restaurant on San Francisco Street, just off the famous Route 66. We had a late lunch and got to know each other a little better. I liked his smile and his gentle blue gray eyes that were full of kindness.

As we spoke about living in Sedona and my arrival there, I noticed that he had a little twinkle in his eye, not only because he probably knew something I didn't, but because it seemed there were little people around him, devas or fairy people, who were ready to get into mischief or play a funny trick on me, or someone else nearby. (I knew of these mischievous beings since I was young, when my father used to speak of them, but also after living in England years earlier, where stories of fairy people playing tricks on others is an accepted truth not just a legend). Too quickly, however, we saw it was getting late so we left the restaurant, found his car nearby and drove back down the canyon.

Everything Robert did was done more slowly than my way. He drove more thoughtfully, he walked more slowly and he seemed to observe the world around him more carefully. I watched everything he did, recognizing that he was different. Then we arrived at his trailer and said our goodbyes. I found my car and drove home, ready to contemplate all that happened for me on this unusual day.

A few days passed before Robert and I talked again, when he dropped by my house. We sat in the nice sunken living room to talk, I on the edge of the beige couch, he on the medium sized brown chair opposite.

It was while we were in the middle of a discussion, catching up on things that happened since we last saw each other when, curiously, he paused in the middle of a sentence. Pointing to a pale-colored dish on the table between us he said, "Let's try something. Look more deeply into this dish and see if you can see its source energy. "

Wondering why he gave me such an exercise, I looked in to see what I could and reported back, "Well I see some unusual particles moving around as if they're floating inside." Satisfied, he then focused on another object nearby and asked me to do the same. Inspired by my responses, he told me that he wanted to continue teaching me things, because I was quick and seemed gifted in seeing a depth to these objects that normally would seem so unimportant.

Not understanding at the moment, I later realized that he had begun a thread of exercises that might help give me another perspective about how different things might look, at their source.

Soon after a sound began patting on the roof, so we both stood up to look out the window. It had started to rain. The sound got louder as drops fell more heavily. Then rolling thunder noises inspired me to open the door. Immediately my eyes followed a horizontal current of lightning flash across the sky before continuous streaks of lightning began flashing everywhere.

We both had the same idea and spontaneously moved the outdoor chairs in front of the house under the overhanging roof so we could watch the lightning hit the ground. It felt like the gods were chasing each other across the skies in some kind of celestial game.

We witnessed endless lightning patterns, from vertical strikes to horizontal ones in more designs than I could ever have imagined.
We "Oooooed" and "Aaaaed" together in response, agreeing that it was better than any fireworks. Shortly after Robert declared that Arizona's annual monsoon season had officially begun.

Already from my short stay in Sedona, I could feel how refreshing the rain was in this dry desert climate. I had watched as my hair lost all its curl the day after my arrival. More significant, however, was my skin's response to the dryness. Days earlier after running my hand down my leg, it felt as if I were touching a fine-grained piece of sandpaper that needed an instant remedy, a daily one in fact.

Driving down the road toward Sedona's many canyons a few days later Robert wanted me to experience the magnetic energies of his favorite place. After parking his car in a small dirt lot we got out, crossed the road and walked on the path toward the high table-shaped rock formation called Doe Mesa. Robert raised his arm up to point out a high mountain lion's cave near the top. When he brought his hand back down, he placed it over mine. I responded, smiling at him as we continued walking hand in hand along the path. My heart was feeling deeper emotions for him; we were becoming more than just friends.

He brought me here so I could experience the feminine energy, the magnetic energy, explaining that it was different from the masculine electrical energy. Several times I stopped to stand alone, and one time it felt as if a pair of arm-like wings were being wrapped around me, warming my heart.

"Yes" I replied after Robert later suggested we have dinner somewhere with an outdoor terrace so we could watch the sunset together. *A nice romantic proposition,* I thought to myself as we walked back to the car. Arriving at my house, he sat on the back terrace in my favorite chair while I changed clothes.

Curiously, my praying mantis friend was still around but had moved to a side window. Looking closer at her, I noticed that her underbelly was back to a normal size and quickly saw her tiny new family members perched on the bark of a nearby tree.

We arrived at the restaurant and were directed to a small isolated table apart from the others where we could watch the sunset and each have a good view. But soon I noticed something moving around in Robert's hair. A closer look revealed two baby praying mantises trying to accommodate themselves; they must have jumped into his hair while he was sitting on my terrace. When I mentioned this to him he smiled and we both stood up, walked over to a nearby tree and transferred them onto an extended branch. Later I looked over to watch where each had found its spot.

We ordered dinner, mine a hazelnut-crusted halibut which became my new favorite fish dish and Robert ordered salmon. While we waited, the sun began its descent below the horizon as the colors of the sky, subtle at first, turned to pinks then to reds. In this eloquent setting I began to ask him questions, wanting to know more details about his life.

"How did you get into channeling" I began. He mused quietly for a minute then answered, "I wanted to have a better understanding of what life was all about, because there's not a lot of communication between parents and their children, to explain life's deeper mysteries."

Then he gave examples of several situations in his life, the first when he was saved from drowning at the age of eleven during a summer boy's camp. Just a short boy then, he went out too far from shore and couldn't get back. Calling out for help, no one heard him; then he blacked out and sunk down into the waters.

He re-awoke realizing that some mysterious being had brought him onto the beach. It was an angel who saved him, he thought. Continuing, he said, "At age nine or ten I had an experience with an extraterrestrial being," and assured me that it was a very positive experience that continued to happen a lot in his life. "It allowed me to be an ambassador for all beings," he said, "and that it is not about losing control, but about having unconditional love for all people, getting along with all people."

I'd heard the term "extraterrestrial" mentioned before and was curious about it, but always left those experiences for others to have, not me. Now however they were coming closer, especially after what Robert just said. In fact he alerted me later that praying mantises were reputed to be another form of an extraterrestrial race exploring earth.

Jokingly I mentioned to him earlier that I thought it was his 6'4" height which allowed him to see things others could not, but after hearing these life experiences, I was a little embarrassed.

He spoke of his life being about helping others understand the ancient mysteries hidden within themselves for which they had found no access. Then he explained that an important part of his core beliefs was that people experience life from their heart.

A light went off in my brain when I realized that, undoubtedly, Robert was to be my new guide. Then several days later he demonstrated a heart exercise for me out on the land.

"Stand in a clear spot with a view of the Red Rocks in every direction," Robert began as I found a place on an elevated rock. "Now turn slowly in either direction and notice when your heart gets warm." I turned slowly looking at each rock carefully until one stopped me. My heart did indeed begin to get warm and then continued to get warmer. Noticing that I had stopped turning, he continued, "Now let the warmth flow into you and listen to any words that come forth."

I stood with my heart warm and feelings of a deep inner peace. Then I said to him, "That rock over there makes my heart get warm. How long should I stay here? It feels like I've received all it wants to give me, but I haven't received any words yet."

Robert replied, "That's fine this is just a beginning. You can do more later and you'll have many different experiences." I was really excited by this seemingly simple exercise, sensing that it would keep me connected to nature, the land and rocks around me no matter where I was.

It took a long time before I realized that Robert's attentiveness in every moment was not only to what was happening around him physically, but to what was happening in other realms as well, in other dimensions with which he was in constant communication. It fascinated me so I often asked for details.

We did many things together, but because Robert had lived with an unusual heart rhythm for most of his life, he couldn't walk too steep a hike or too far. So, if I wanted to take a longer, steeper hike, I did it myself.

Luckily, soon after arriving in Sedona, I met a woman named Sandra, who became an immediate good friend. We went out on the land together a lot and she taught me things as well. I called her my "medicine sister."

Too soon however, my time had slipped by and two months had passed. I had already extended my stay into early September, but now I was being called back to upstate New York. I had received a large grant to bring a two-week holography program into a school at the end of September, so I had to go.

Robert and I were now in a gentle passionate relationship and he often stayed with me, at my house, if he didn't have any early morning clients. I loved the way he helped friends better understand difficult situations in their lives. He was compassionate and I valued most everything he said.

With my departure time days away, he suggested we have dinner in a small cozy family restaurant. It was a Friday and they were having the all-you-can-eat ribs special that we liked so much. We'd been there several times together.

After ordering we were silent a moment. Robert looked over at me in a sideways glance with his soft blue-gray eyes. He took my hand and then turned to face me more directly. Smoothly he delivered his question, "Will you marry me?"

As if I'd just entered a dream I remembered seeing a shooting star streak across the heavenly cosmos. It was the evening I drove past Lake George, New York, two days before I left for the southwest. A thought popped into my head about wanting to get married. Then in that same moment, a shooting star streaked across the vast night sky. Perhaps my dream was coming true.

Then I focused back on Robert. He was not looking at me but facing down toward the table waiting for my answer. The waitress arrived to deliver our dinner salads and placed them on the table one in front of each of us, then turned and left. Being unprepared for his question I lingered on it.

I'd had several partners for five or more years each, but I never had a proposal, realizing that maybe I never wanted one. My photography career with lots of teaching and later my holography career had taken all my time.

Finally, lifting my head to look at him more directly, I cleared my throat to give him my answer, "Yes Robert, I will." My heart got warm, expanded, as we smiled and raised our wine glasses to celebrate, gazing at each other shyly. I was happy, surprised, never expecting anything like this to actually happen.

We talked and made a plan for what we would do next. After finishing my two week holography program in the upstate school, I would pack up all my belongings, complete my relationships with all the schools around New York State and my work with Adirondack Life Magazine, then sell most of my furniture. Robert would fly out to Albany, New York and we would drive back to Sedona together.

And that was exactly what we did. I brought some things with me on the drive, but I sent a few larger pieces of furniture by a truck to Sedona.

Then Robert and I would get married when the time felt right. It would be the beginning of my new life.

Chapter 5 – A New Life

Living in a place so beautiful was hard to believe. Unmistakably, life was turning in a new direction as Robert and I moved into our apartment. Luckily, Robert found a nice two-story duplex just before he flew to meet me in New York.

While unpacking after our long cross-country drive, we realized the need for some new furniture. Our first purchase was an off-white couch, a love seat that Robert chose, which seemed unusual for such a tall person; it would be like a giant sitting on a child's couch. But days later he revealed why. "If ever we have a disagreement or get upset with each other," he began with that mischievous gleam in his eyes, "and sit on this couch, our love seat, close, it could resolve the issue. It would remind us of our true feelings for each other." I was touched.

He brought over a small end table from his trailer to put on one side of the couch and his dresser for the bedroom. Then we bought a bed for tall people. My hutch finally arrived from back east, slightly damaged, but it was the only piece of furniture I'd found that fit all my photography prints from shows and my thousands of 35 millimeter negatives (when we used reflex cameras) from my long career.

Kindly, Robert suggested I have the second upstairs bedroom, as I had more "stuff" than he and it might help me adjust to the life-changing move, having never lived as far from the east coast (excluding the two years living in France with the French peasant farmers).

Conveniently we also found a nice wood dining room table to put close by the kitchen area, in the dining room, where Robert would do his client sessions. It gave our new home a cozy feeling.

Robert had evenings when he did channeling for the public where I met new people, including the owner of *The Sedona Journal.* She published many of his channeling sessions in her magazine, which also featured other people's channeled articles.

Sometimes we walked to the calm waters of Oak Creek together to my favorite spot at Red Rock Crossing in front of Cathedral Rock. Or we sat up at the airport vortex area, where Robert also liked to go alone. Often he would be there for hours communicating with beings from different realms. He was connected to realms where most people would be afraid to go, except for those who came to Sedona, anticipating journeys into these *unknown territories*. I had been one of them.

There were many experiential possibilities offered in this small mystical town. I had learned some things about metaphysics and the psychic world with my teacher in his New York school. But after being in such a heightened energetic place, surrounded by these enchanting Red Rocks, I became more and more open, almost too sensitive.

Sedona was known for its vortices, which I learned, according to geologists, were electro-magnetic energies that seeped out from the deep fissures or cracks in the earth and spun either to the right or to the left. Many who came to Sedona learned how these energies could help clear unresolved emotions or life patterns if they sat and meditated in a vortex. Native American people understood them, but most other people did not, so they came from far and near to experience them.

Two weeks before Robert's and my first summer solstice together on June 21st, the message came from my inner voice—a voice I was hearing more from these days—that it was the moment for us to get married. I quickly informed both my sisters, one on the east coast, the other on the west coast, who came to support me. The small ceremony would be at the top of Schnebly Hill, (when we could still drive up the winding, rutted, ascent to the top without needing a high clearance vehicle). Accompanied by my sisters and a few other friends, we arrived at this special breathtaking overlook.

An older woman and friend of Robert would marry us. She was one of the original women of Sedona who drove the first pink jeep, which inspired an entire tour company.

Underneath a sturdy wide alligator juniper tree, with full branches stretched out in every direction, we had our ceremony. I brought my beige and red woven Navajo wedding basket to hold the rings we had a Hopi man create, mine with a deer print in it.

Quietly, as soon as our items were gathered and we were ready, tears began falling from my eyes and I began to cry softly. It was from a place deep inside that lasted for several minutes. But in this delicate moment I had no choice but wait until it stopped.

Lastly, as soon as the official part was over, after we read our vows to each other, Robert kissed me. One friend took a photo. Days later when we saw it, there was a rainbow arched across our faces. It was magical.

We had a simple reception at a friend's home where more people came to celebrate with us before we departed on our honeymoon to Lake Powell in northern Arizona. It was a place I'd never been.

Intentionally flooded many years previous to create a recreational lake, ancient Navajo canyons and special caves had been submerged under the water. Our hotel overlooked this vast lake.

It was on our first night that Robert became aware of trapped beings beneath the waters that were crying out for his help. Luckily these lost spirits knew how to contact him from other realms, the ones I began realizing he knew so well.

Thus instead of laughing and frolicking mindlessly in the waters the way other people were doing, that one might imagine on a honeymoon, he spent a day attempting to free these trapped spirits.

A new experience for me, I witnessed how Robert responded to the situation. He could hear the spirits' call from beneath the waters and explained how they had been trapped in the caves when this man-made lake was created.

Then I began to feel their distress coming from somewhere as I followed Robert to the waters edge and then to one of the inlets around Lake Powell. He called in higher spirits that he sometimes worked with to assist, but I wasn't certain who they were and what reality they were from.

After Robert did what he could to help them, sending them to a higher place so their souls could continue to evolve on their personal journeys, he said, we rented a small boat and went out onto the lake. This was our moment of honoring our marriage commitment together. But I wondered if one day I too would receive a mission to help other beings from a binding situation. Curiously, this experience was the beginning of our new life together.

Several weeks after the honeymoon, we were walking together when I had the most important experience from any of Robert's teachings. Behind the famous Bell Rock area known to be an electrical vortex where many spoke of seeing or hearing about UFO visitations, there is a path. It is between Bell Rock and Courthouse Rock.

Each is a magnificently created rock structure. Bell Rock, smaller, is circular like a merry-go-round of red rocks that spiral up to a spire at its tallest peak. Courthouse Rock has a much larger circumference with a rougher, thicker circular shape around which are several standing rock forms. It seemed like they could be guardians for an inner temple that might exist within.

Continuing slowly down the path between these two distinct rock formations, Robert stopped, faced Courthouse Rock and gave me an exercise to do. "Take these two fingers on your right hand just so*,* " as he stood facing it. He stretched two fingers out toward Courthouse Rock, "and aim them at this massive butte, allowing them to take you in to see more deeply what is there, inside.*"* Then he dropped his hand and turned to watch me do it.

I did the exercise he demonstrated, whereby my two fingers quickly gave me access inside the mystical butte, where my inner vision saw details of a well formed crystal room, perhaps a temple, with a circular staircase of soft purple amethyst hugging the side walls. It rose up from the bottom allowing a person to walk along the periphery of the inside temple here.

In disbelief that an exercise so simple could bring me such immediate knowledge, I related my experience, without totally understanding it, when Robert urged me to trust what I thought came only from my imagination. He said that it was my inner knowing, my inner seeing and to not be afraid of it. "It is real and now you can go from there, learn more details everywhere you go, into canyons, on rock walls or explore dense rock formations to look more deeply into unimaginable sources there."

Grateful, inspired, I practiced this exercise everywhere I went, looking into ponds or rock formations, while I was out alone on a walk or exploring new areas with a friend. I practiced trusting my inner vision as I explored into these *otherworlds*.

However, back in the three dimensional, physical world, I began to examine the money-making part of my life. Yes, I had changed my life by moving to the southwest and marrying my new husband, but aside from the beauty of the red rocks and these new teachings, my mind still wanted to know what my new life's purpose was.

While waiting to know more, I decided to continue doing what I 'd done in my past, offering holography presentations around Arizona and New Mexico in different schools. I also began resurrecting a dream I'd had, while working in the photographic world.

I had done a story for an upstate New York magazine on *The Adirondack Cowboy*, but when I wanted to follow it with a second story on the *Cowgirl*, they thought it was too soon. So I waited. To me, the cowgirl was the untold story; she was carrying an aspect of the feminine whose deeper story had not yet been told – not in the proper depth.

Now, in the perfect location of the southwest, I began to pursue this dream of traveling around photographing cowgirls riding wild bulls and broncs. I also found a few longtime ranching women as I began photographing.

It took me all around the southwest, to the "Cowgirl Hall of Fame" in Texas and then to California documenting the last female "trick" riders. I traveled to Idaho and photographed a famous "Hall of Fame" bronc riding woman on her ranch and then to many Indian reservations where I found very young girls age four and five riding on sheep. Their goal was to one day ride wild horses or bulls, when they were old enough.

As far as most people were concerned, cowgirls were a legend in the US; they were the ones who freed the spirit of all women and changed the tradition of wearing dresses and skirts. Pants were the more practical option when riding wild horses or untamed bulls at the turn of the century in America's history. I learned a lot.

After a few years of doing holography in southwest schools, it became obvious that the teachers were not interested in learning how to do it themselves, getting their own equipment, as with my upstate New York schools, even with my guidance. So I stopped teaching it.

Having completed my longtime photographic dream of following and documenting cowgirls, I felt I was being called in another direction. I stopped photographing on any more long term projects.

Chapter 6 – The Shamanic Worlds

Longing, there was a longing deep inside me that was calling. Ever since the floating diamond vehicle had appeared outside my balcony window with that angelic being inside, my heart had been calling out. After having experienced what otherworldly relationships could be like I wanted to know more.

Robert had assisted me in working with individual spirits in nature, those of trees, rocks and of the waters, which helped me understand the interrelationships, but I wanted to have more.

As soon as my friend Sandra mentioned meeting personal guides in other realities during a shamanic journey, I wanted to learn about it. Maybe this was the time to observe the world from a different perspective, one I had never known before.

Sandra learned to do shamanic journeys a year earlier and informed me of workshops sponsored by the *Foundation for Shamanic Studies*. It was an organization founded by an anthropologist who spent his life studying indigenous people's shamanic practices around the planet which he then put into what he called "core shamanism."

Excited, I quickly learned that Foundation teachers traveled around the US making these workshops available. Surprisingly, two weeks later there was one being offered in Phoenix south of Sedona, so I eagerly signed up.

Basic Shamanism was a two-day first level class, which taught the shamanic journey techniques and was an opportunity to meet my first spirit guide. It was a facilitated by a woman who lived in Santa Fe.

When I entered the large conference room with my notebook in hand and my blanket over my arm, it seemed primitive that everyone was gathered on the floor. Some people were sitting on mats, while others brought blankets to lie on; I quickly learned that shamans always did their work on the ground.

A short slim woman with long dark hair and brown eyes sat in the middle with her drum. She began, telling us that shamanism is the oldest spiritual practice in the world going back more than 100,000 years, when shamans had to develop ways of working with disharmony and dis-ease.

I learned that shamanism offered an opportunity to access hidden dimensions and unseen allies who were devoted to our healing and evolution. They could help us navigate our life she told us, not only in pursuit of a career or love perspective, but to one of fulfilling our greater purpose

Oh my, I thought to myself after hearing these words, *I have indeed come to the right place.*

I remember her saying: "As you develop skills to journey into different worlds, like the upper, middle or lower, it depends on the information you seek. For instance by journeying to the upper world you might meet a teacher who could appear as a goddess, an angel or a long departed ancestor. By going to the lower world you might meet a power animal."

She explained that journeying is about leaving this reality, as you go into another one, in an altered state of consciousness. A drumbeat leads you to this place where the spirits take over and possibly offer you life-changing wisdom.

Our first day, we would be journeying to the lower world, the inner earth, to meet one of our spirit animals. Evidently it was a shamanic belief that when a person is born, he or she has three protecting animal guides, each carrying a different quality. Our first protocol was to set an intention to go there.

The next protocol was choosing a doorway, an entrance place into this lower world, perhaps a tunnel or cave, a waterfall or tree trunk, something that was familiar.

As the continuous drumming began, I was lying down with my eyes closed. Anxious, my mind began to search for a way to enter. I was afraid to go into a cave or into water on this first journey, afraid I might get stuck there and not be able to get out. Trying to relax, I remembered a nice tree outside the apartment, not tall and thick, but short with many branches. So I choose this tree.

Quickly, my consciousness shifted to another place as I saw myself approach the tree trunk. Finding filaments of a fibrous root-like substance inside the trunk, I slid down them into the *lower world*. My arrival place was on a dirt pathway in a softly lit area.

We were told that various animals would appear to us, but the one who wanted to speak to us would appear four times. Then we'd know it was the one. It might give us information or we might ask a question before the return drumbeat called us back. We needed to return the same way we had entered.

Indeed, different animals began appearing to me, a mountain goat, then a deer, walking along one side of the path, on my right, then again on my left, before a mountain lion passed by in front of me.

Then the mountain lion passed by again, and suddenly it appeared on the trail facing me. Quickly I turned to look behind me and also saw it standing there.

OK, this must be my animal, I thought, but before I was given its name a message was already coming to me: *Take the clutter out of your life and start simplifying things; simplicity is clarity. Stop worrying about achieving, it is time for you to be in your body and to take responsibility for your life.*

When I thought the mountain lion had finished, not so, there was more, *It is time to reclaim yourself and see yourself as a whole woman as you wish to be. You are not a victim to anything.* And with that, the message was complete.

Mountain Lion came up to me on the path after, assuring me, telepathically, that she (it felt like the gender was feminine) would give me advice as I needed it.

Suddenly, I heard the drumbeat change and thanked her quickly, anxious to hurry back. After traveling through the same tree trunk, I felt my consciousness return to my body lying in the Phoenix hotel conference room, just as the last drumbeat sounded.

Some people shared their journey details, but I was already processing Mountain Lion's message to me. Evidently it was common practice after meeting our power animal, to dance as if we were that animal. So we danced them, helping to seal the connection.

Our facilitator drummed as everyone moved around the room, some slithering along the floor as snakes, others making occasional leaps through the air as a deer or elk might move. Others appeared to be birds in flight with their arms moving as wings. Me, I was on my four new legs walking awkwardly straight ahead, my mouth wide howling in a loud catlike meow. I wanted to honor my new animal ally.

The workshop served me well as it began a lifelong calling into shamanism. I bought a drum and continued to journey, taking other classes. My friend Sandra began a drumming group that met weekly as I journeyed to new worlds, the upper and middle where I met new guides and teachers.

Feeling supported by this work, if I had questions about people or my own life situations I could journey and ask my guides for answers.

Shortly after I was accepted into the three year advanced program at the Foundation for Shamanic Studies, considered the most advanced program anywhere. It would continue my initiations in shamanism. There were two one-week sessions, one in the spring, the other in the fall, for three years, during which I learned far more than I would ever use.

Years later I recognized that I was able to travel into places easily without a drum journey, see into other worlds and realities. However, one journey I liked practicing if I noticed my attitude getting arrogant or lacking compassion. It was called a "dis-memberment journey."

In it, I would go down to the lower world to meet my spirit animals, who often engaged other helpers in the most seemingly heart-wrenching methods to dissolve me into nothingness. I never knew what they would be doing to get me out of my mind, back into my heart. I accepted whatever they chose to do for me.

I remember one time, after setting my intention *to be dis-membered*, I went down into the lower world, passing first through the tree roots, which quickly took me onto my usual path in the other world, where my mountain lion animal guide met me. Then a puma came over to join it and other kinds of cats arrived. Larger beings began to come over, a wolf and a tall white winged being who hovered above me, as other tall winged bird-like beings came over and surrounded me.

Suddenly, with an unexpected swipe of someone's paw or wing, my head came off. I was a body without a head, before one of the winged beings reached in and took out my heart, then another picked out my organs.

Two snakes wrapped around each one of my legs, while a third one wrapped itself around my stomach and the middle part of my body. Suddenly, my body disappeared. It was gone.

Where am I, Where am I, I kept asking, again and again, as I heard my inner voice cry out, feeling that I was somewhere that felt good, but I couldn't see any physical body.

Lastly, after successfully being dissolved, my inner voice requested, *I want to be 're-membered,' please put me back together into 'something.'*

Watching, I saw myself begin as a particle of light, which then became or formed into what looked like a goddess figure wearing a white and gold speckled gown. I had a crown of stars on my head. It felt wonderful being merged into gold and white particles of light. Fascinated, it appeared that I had become this being, a new essence of myself. I wondered if my perception would begin to happen through this being's eyes?

Chapter 7 – She Appears

Weeks had passed since my first workshop in shamanism, as I sat in my favorite place by the water, isolated. The creek flowed effortlessly in pursuit of its own unknown destination as the refreshing sounds quieted my busy mind.

I was humbled by the majestic view of the red rocks in front of me as I took a moment to reflect on the magic that had greeted my arrival. Not sure if they were visions or reality, I saw rainbows floating everywhere, touching trees, arching across the high red rock pinnacles in the distance, as I drove into the dusty parking lot at Red Rock Crossing. Hurrying, I locked the car door, slid my arms through my backpack straps, and walked toward these floating rainbows. Sadly, they dissolved with each step I took, but I hoped they would re-appear.

Walking over to sit on my favorite rock by the water, I drifted off into a light meditation. Comfortable, I could have stayed there for hours focused inward and away from my busy thoughts from the outer world.

A wisp-like breeze swirled around me gently, then stopped. Then again I felt the same swirl around me, playing with my hair before it stopped. A third time I felt the same wisp-like breeze.

Finally, I realized something might be trying to get my attention. Very still, I looked in using my shamanic vision. Yes, there it was, a mystical light hovering a short distance away from me. My eyes still closed but discerning carefully, I saw a feminine figure dressed in a light colored garment. She beckoned me to follow her.

I watched in this otherworld as the rays of light that surrounded her, mysteriously started shining on me. Being able to step into these inner worlds was like walking down some road with no sign of a destination. It was like I was moving on some edgeless path leading to nowhere I had ever known.

Other women soon came into view dressed in white gowns from which these rays of light were emanating. They quickly surrounded me in a circle when, mysteriously, their light broke down to become individually colored beams, like those you would find in a rainbow.

I watched this new kind of "cinema" as it displayed a circle of women before me who quickly demonstrated how they could also become standing stones, telepathically telling me that I could call on them for support if ever necessary. I was curious to know how they could support me as a standing stone or a beam of light.

Just minutes after this scene had been displayed the feminine figure spoke words to me telepathically, saying:

A woman has to find her center in order to find out and know who she is. Mountains are a source of feminine power, because the great mother offers her fire to the mountains and it will always bring you home to her, heart to heart.

I listened as if she were an oracle to whom I was coming for council, wondering if I really understood what she was telling me, when she got more specific, more personal, saying:

It is time for you to transfer some of your energy and trust from that of the male to that of the female.

Interestingly, in my early life, my father often played both roles for me, the mother as well as the father, after my mother was diagnosed with a mental disorder.

A lot of emotions came up that took me back to my early childhood, to the experience of father and mother, my first archetypes of the male and female roles in this life. Her message was asking me to cleanse many things within my belief systems, so I would be able to accept and open to my inner female self. She continued:

And being open to receive is an important part of walking the path of the feminine.

Immediately I felt the circle of women surround me, as standing stones, beams of light, and knew they had already begun to support me. *Was this a call to begin walking the path of the feminine*, I asked myself? I wondered if there was a way to get onto the feminine path, to learn more about it.

Months passed after having this experience, when, the word *goddess* and *priestess* came up during a celebration on New Year's Eve. I had gone alone to the party, because Robert preferred to stay home, as he was working on a project.

Here, I met two Sedona women talking about a trip they were offering to Glastonbury, England the following May. It was a journey to experience the feminine spirit during the ancient cross-quarter festival called "Beltane" on May 1st, in the ancient Goddess traditions of Glastonbury, England.

They explained how this specific time of the year symbolized the Earth's waking up, as the weather got warmer and her seeds began to grow again inside the earth. I was intrigued, because I too was ready to "wake up" and invite the long lost seeds of my own feminine spirit to blossom.

The two women spoke of several places they would visit that could possibly impact a person's perspective on life: the Chalice Well, the Glastonbury Tor, the world's first and oldest Abbey, and other places including several famous stone circles. After I heard this, it was like a spark of lightning had ignited me inside so I immediately committed myself to go on this trip.

Lastly, minutes after leaving this New Years Eve event and opening my car door, I sat down ready to turn on the ignition key when something stopped me.

Out of nowhere a dark speckled snake appeared raising itself up in front of me as if a hidden doorway had opened wide and let it out. Seeming very alive it wavered back and forth in front of my face, looking directly into my eyes as its long sleek neck stretched itself out, its gray piercing eyes locked into mine.

I couldn't move my face away from it because of my limited space. I had to stay in my seat. Then, shockingly, a stream of spit left the snake's curved mouth and fell around my eyes.

Stunned, instinctively my fingers reached for a tissue from the nearby box in the car to wipe it off. It seemed to be dripping down my cheeks. After wiping it I looked to see, but there was nothing on my tissue.

Did this actually happen, I asked myself *Was this some kind of initiation*? Curiously, ever since this moment, snakes and I have been connected, having encounters on the land, in rocks, but most often while sitting in nature near water.

Nothing was ever the same after my commitment to going on the Glastonbury trip; it marked the beginning of my personal journey to walk and understand the *path of the feminine.*

Chapter 8 - Glastonbury

Following the call, women began traveling thousands of miles across continents and vast oceans to arrive at the ancient place known as Glastonbury, in Somerset, England, as if they were returning to their place of origin. The Goddess tradition was being revived, honored and celebrated there again openly.

We were a group of thirteen women, mostly from Sedona, who had indeed traveled across oceans and continents to arrive in Glastonbury ready to deepen our connection with the feminine spirit, the *Goddess,* as they called her in Glastonbury, although Avalon was the town's earlier name.

In her book, *Priestess of Avalon, Priestess of the Goddess*, Kathy Jones says, "The Goddess and women's spirituality is an unwritten book that women are attempting to redress now in these times. We begin to hear her speak to us with no human mediator between ourselves, and her, no priest standing between us and the divine, no book that tells us what to believe, who we are and how to be....We re-create from our souls now, in the present.... to bring our innate divinity to life again at last." [1]

Coming straight from the London airport, we arrived in Glastonbury. On a road that passed by its highest hill, I noticed a distinguishable ruin on the top that was surrounded by the brightest green grass I'd seen in years, coming from Arizona's high deserts. It was known as the Glastonbury Tor.

Our facilitators Liz and Anne began giving us details about the legend that at the foot of this Glastonbury Tor might be where Joseph of Arimathea buried the Holy Grail Cup from Jesus' Last Supper when he came here 2000 years ago. And it was suggested to be the reason why Glastonbury's famous well was called the "Chalice Well." And then we were told Joseph requested an Abbey be built here.

As our bus glided down to the bottom of the famous High Street, the one main street going through the town, we passed the entrance to this Abbey, the Glastonbury Abbey. Today it is known to be the oldest above ground Christian church in the world, Liz told us, but only a ruin now with its grounds still occupying the main part of Glastonbury.

Continuing up this steep main street, I noticed the quaint stores on each side, bakeries, bookstores and restaurants, before we finally reached our hotel at the top.

Called the Chalice Hill House, it was a tall, elegant, white building, probably from the turn of the century, with high ceilings and graciously proportioned rooms.

Tired from our overnight flights, as soon the van parked, we all found our suitcases, carried them up the wide staircase to our rooms, so we could relax and settle in a little. Most of us shared rooms. The one my roommate and I had was small, upstairs in the back, but it had a wonderful view of the hill behind through an oval window.

Later, we all gathered to learn a few details, including breakfast times, before most of us went to bed, ready to catch up from our eight-hour time difference.

The first day, I came down the wide Victorian staircase a little early to be alone for a few minutes outside the hotel's front door. I wanted to gaze out over

Glastonbury and muse on the legendary places we would be experiencing. One place I would miss however, after reading about it in the *Mists of Avalon*, by Marion Zimmer Bradley, was now only a timeless legend. Long ago a priestess temple sat at the waters edge, in the southern part of the town where legends claimed people stopped, often for a night. It was before they crossed over to the island in the middle, thousands of years ago, when Glastonbury, the Celtic word for the "Isle Of Glass", was surrounded by water.

Bradley explained that its earlier name was *Avalon,* when it was called 'the place of the apples', and thought to be where the 'golden apples of immortality' could be found. Curiously, it was also this temple in the Arthurian legends where King Arthur came for healing after being wounded in battle by his son Mordred.

Evidently, she said, not only was the temple situated at the entranceway to this sacred isle, but it had been built around an ancient well dedicated to the Goddess Brigid, known to have lived here and to whom, evidently, the earlier peoples once came for healing. I fantasized it, sitting outside the hotel, imagining this elusive temple.

Slowly group members began coming down for breakfast, one by one, so I took one last glance at the landscape and turned to go back inside. I loved how we were served the traditional English breakfast of fried tomatoes, eggs, bacon and toast. It was not only tasty, but seemed essential in preparing us for the frosty spring mornings of late April.

After finishing, we gathered together in the living room and officially began our journey. Each woman was invited to talk about why she had come, as we sat around in a circle on couches and a few stuffed chairs. When it was my turn, I began by saying that my life seemed to be going to a new place, from a different perspective. It was not just about assuming that I was a woman and leading my life the way most women had done before with a husband, children; it was something else.

It began after a mystical feminine figure appeared to me, saying that it is time for me to reclaim something that has been lost deep within me. Now I wanted to know what that was and why my life has been without it. Finally, I admitted that I had no idea what I was looking for, that this was my first journey or pilgrimage to anywhere.

Most of the women had similar quests, wanting to see these famous sites, but also to share it and have fun with other women. Once each had spoken, we were told we would begin our journey by walking over to the Chalice Well, next to our hotel.

Everybody quickly ran to their rooms to prepare for the cool weather, so I put on my jacket, beret and warm boots. As soon as everyone was gathered, we walked across the hotel lawn to a narrow dirt path leading to a low metal gate that separated the two properties.

After passing through this gate, we were officially at the top of the Chalice Well Garden. I passed bushes along the path pregnant with buds ready to burst open in possible colors of pink, yellow or deep purple, as we moved down toward the well.

Unexpectedly, I felt something change as we continued down this path. My entire body began to shiver, starting from behind my heart then moving down both my arms. Aware of a feeling that we were spiraling down toward something that seemed hidden from physical view, it was almost as if we had stepped through some kind of veiled doorway.

Arriving at the famous Chalice Well, we were guided to step down into the sunken area surrounding it, paved with smooth flat rocks laid carefully into the dirt.

We were fifteen women standing around this most ancient well site. Seeming to be timeless, I imagined it extended back thousands of years through many disguises. It felt so right, like we had just entered into some kind of eternal presence that lingered above us, as if it had always been here and would continue after we were gone.

A gentle loving energy was coming up from the well, encased by its circular stone design, so I stretched over to peer down at the water. It was too far down to touch, but I liked seeing the small ferns growing along the sides just above the water.

A round iron cover protecting the well was open, constructed with a symbol of two circles slightly overlapping that were viewable while it was either open or closed. We learned that some referred to it as a *vesica pisces* and that the man who created it in 1919 had envisioned it as a symbol of the inner and outer worlds interlocking.

Both Liz and Anne offered prayers for the journey and for the wellbeing of each of us, finishing with words of gratitude to Brigid, the ancient guardian here. Brigid was the most well-known goddess figure in the British Isles, they told us and from which the word "Britannia" originated. It helped me understand more about her once living at the priestess temple here.

Savoring the sacred moment, we stood quietly connected to each other by our joined hands. Then we followed where the water flowed to where it came out a fountain sculpted like a lion's head. I saw people drink the waters flowing from its mouth. A rusty red colored stone, tinted from the iron in the water, lay beneath this fountain, with a cup nearby, available for anyone wanting to drink.

Slowly, I proceeded down the paved pathway, the green grass on each side and unscrewed my bottle top to catch the flowing water from the lion's mouth. After a few gulps, I could taste the iron in it. Iron oxide deposits gave it not only the slight red tint, but also the slight iron taste that evidently was compared to a women's menstrual blood.

Then we followed the water's path, and one by one moved carefully down the short span of steps beside a tiny rock hill, where the waters flowed into a narrow open stream-like place, where people could bathe their feet.

Feeling suddenly giddy, in a childlike moment after descending these steps, I broke off several tiny pieces of chocolate from a bar I had with me. I left them on small stones half hidden by greenery next to where the water flowed. They were gifts for the fairies, those little people I'd heard about since I was young, who lived in the flower worlds. I was sure they lived here.

Lastly, we followed the water on its final path between two slightly twisted old yew trees, which must have marked some ancient ceremonial place. Here it flowed down into two large circular ponds overlapping, exactly as it was designed on the Chalice Well cover. Each was filled with the flowing well waters.

While our group was proceeding down to these two ponds we fell into a single line, one behind the other, when suddenly I had a memory of myself being here and doing this before.

Priestesses, we were following one behind the other in a line and each woman was wearing a long flowing white dress. As this ancient memory took me over, I unmistakably saw columns of light coming down from above, transporting something into the top of each woman's head, as if she suddenly became a column of light. It began to stir something inside me, as I became more conscious of this possibility, moving back and forth between the two different worlds.

When the vision stopped I was back in the present moment and joined the group standing next to the two circular ponds. It seemed to be a more public gathering place, where we learned that larger ceremonies were held. I saw people entering the Chalice Well Garden here, through a small door in the outer wall, where there was also a gift shop.

On our journey, we visited other places too, which included the famous stone circles, Avebury and then Stonehenge, but our late April journey was synchronized so we could celebrate the traditional pagan festival called *Beltane* on May 1st; May Day as we call it in America.

When nature wakes up after a long winter of sleep in the spring, she is ready for 'her' seeds to grow again. It is felt by everything living on the Earth, including humans. Thus it seemed to symbolize a 'time for love' and perhaps is why there are so many weddings in May, I realized.

Liz spoke about how mythologically, *Beltane* was also a time when the doorways were believed to open between our physical world and the *otherworld*, giving access into the hollow hills and the many magical mounds located in Glastonbury.

Glancing around, I could see that Glastonbury had many hills, or mounds, where it was believed these ancient Gods and Goddesses might have retreated, along with other beings, no longer being honored on the earth. Undoubtedly this must have been during the shift, from the matriarchy to that of the patriarchy, thousands of years ago I thought.

Moreover, I was fascinated to learn that our group would be walking around this conical shaped Glastonbury Tor, which was, mysteriously, also known to be a labyrinth. Starting the day before Beltane, we would walk in and then leave that evening. Then the second day, Beltane, May 1st, we would return to walk out. It was a custom here, evidently, to be suspended in the energy overnight.

I had never walked into a labyrinth before, so it would be my first, but I remembered reading that it was an ancient ceremony.

The principal of the Tor Labyrinth was explained to us. It had seven levels, each connected to or identified with one of the seven chakras in the body, beginning with the 1st chakra in the sacral area, then going up to the top of the head, the 7th level. Emotions have been associated with each level, so as one walks the levels, it can clear up or stir up corresponding energy in the body.

Evidently, back in 1265, an earthquake had shifted the *Tor Labyrinth,* making it uneven, one side lower than the other. Thus, it was essential to have a knowledgeable person as a guide, and the well-known Glastonbury author, Kathy Jones would be leading us.

On the morning of our walk, we first gathered at the base of the Tor to be introduced to Kathy. Then together we walked the steep path to the labyrinth entrance.

Leaning against one of the large rocks marking the entrance, Kathy explained the protocol. "It is important to always make an intention before entering any labyrinth, so you know what you're walking into." She then said that you enter all labyrinths on the 3rd level, the place to which she had led us. As we all stood near the large rounded bolder marking the entrance, we were ready to step in, one by one.

Aware of how strong intentions can be, and after some thought, I offered my prayer. "My intention is to go back and connect with and understand more precisely, the ancient lineage of the feminine. I want to know the ancient feminine roots." Then I extended my right foot forward, stepped inside and began my journey.

Around the first terrace, I began my ritual, going to each of the levels, carefully tuned into my body sensations. The conical shape of the Tor made it seem as if I were walking into the womb of the great mother Earth. It wound back and forth, up and down, on the uneven slopes of this ancient pattern, the moist dirt often slippery as I placed each foot carefully in front of me.

Sometimes I might say a few words to someone while on the narrow path, but mostly kept to myself, attuned to what my body might want to tell me. My journey mates seemed to be doing the same.

Curiously, after rounding the final curve of one level, ready to head up to the 4th level, tears started flowing down my face. I sensed a deep sadness as I moved onto the 4th level corresponding to the heart. Slowly, I placed one foot in front of the other, noticing that my heart was experiencing some kind of longing, deep within, wanting to reach out to something mysterious. *What is it?* I tuned into my heart, but I had no response.

Soon after moving down to the lower side of the 4th level, I spotted a yellow jacket bee lying in the grass. I bent over to look closer to see if I could assist. It was heavily laden with pollen and had fallen down, sideways and couldn't get up.

Reaching out my finger, I carefully turned it over so it could right itself and picked it up. The bee rested on my finger, wavering back and forth for a short time, before aiming its body in a steady forward stance, when it courageously flew away.

Then I caught up with the others. After almost three hours we gathered on the 5th level. It was from here we walked out that first night.

However, in the beginning of our labyrinth walk, down on the 1st level, at the base of the Tor, one of the women from Sedona fell to the ground as her body froze up; she couldn't move.

Our facilitator Liz ran over and assessed her situation, saying that it would be best for her to go back to her room and lie down. After two painful days in bed with a high fever, she felt better, probably having cleared something stuck in her lower chakra, whereby Liz then helped her finish walking the labyrinth.

We, the rest of our group, returned that next morning and walked out of the labyrinth, starting from the 5th level where we left it the previous day.

Once again as I turned onto the 4th level, tears flowed from my eyes. It seemed like I was grasping for something deep in my heart, but searching my soul, the thought came that maybe there was something living deep inside this ancient mound, the Tor, upon which I had been walking.

Continuing to walk, up, down, around, I was aware that other people, not from our group, had joined us as we walked out. Briefly, I spoke with one or two of these people while walking the levels.

But one man had a story I couldn't easily forget. Two years previous, he walked into this labyrinth and walked out as we had the previous evening, but something kept him from returning to complete his walk out. Destiny pulled him. He witnessed his whole life fall apart in front of him, as he lost his wife and then his job.

As his life was beginning to come back together, two full years later, he walked out with our group, mentioning that he had to accept what needed to happen. Now, by walking out he hoped to "seal" his new life path. *What a story*, I thought, wondering if I would ever be able to manage an experience like his.

Then I met an American woman, walking out with us, who said she was staying in Glastonbury for several months. We spoke briefly and she mentioned she was going away for a week. I had mentioned visiting Iona Island off the western coast of Scotland after the group journey was over. Thus she, assuming I would need a place to stay in Glastonbury after, offered me her room. I accepted, graciously.

Any wisdom or knowledge that might come from my labyrinth intention, connecting to the ancient lineage of the feminine, I realized, was not going to be downloaded to me in one afternoon, or possibly not even during a ten-day spiritual journey. Moreover, I realized it might take years of experiences, or maybe even one-on-one initiations with unknown beings, before the intention might come back to me.

But, that intention started to become real after my return from Iona, when, once again, I was back in Glastonbury.

Chapter 9 – The Spinning Diamond of Iona

As soon as the women from the Glastonbury group boarded planes to return home, I, and my new friend Christy took a four-day excursion to the Isle of Iona, off the west coast of Scotland. It was considered part of the Inner Hebrides.

Several people were discussing it during our tour, but it was after I heard that the Essenes and maybe Jesus himself had visited Iona, that I wanted to explore it. They said Iona was known as the *Holy Isle.*

We took a train from London to the Scottish town of Oban, then two ferries, the first from Oban to the island of Mull, across it by a bus to the 15 minute ferry for Iona. Then we were there.

Minutes after stepping onto the island, we were both quickly aware of the powerful energies and sensations emanating from the land. It was not from the luscious green grasses or the numerous sheep grazing in the pastures everywhere; the energy sensation seemed, elusively, to be coming from somewhere else.

After we checked into a small country inn, climbed the wooden stairs to our room and had barely let go of our suitcase handles, we both mysteriously collapsed on our beds. It was as if we had taken a heavy dose of some strong drug or drank too much wine and passed out.   Whatever it was the impact took me so deep I could barely move a finger.

Finally I raised my head to see that it was late afternoon and got up, ready to begin exploring the mysterious island with the last light of the day.

I was informed earlier in Glastonbury about a famous Abbey here that Iona carried a great legacy as being an early religious center where several monasteries had been established. Another common legend I heard was that forty-eight kings had been crowned here and that some were buried in the Abbey graveyard, which we explored that first afternoon.

During our next few days, Christy and I chose to walk in the four directions around the island. Late afternoon of our second day, we walked in the westerly direction. Arriving at the end of the path, Christy quickly took the direction straight to the beach because she saw a seal in the water. But I chose a narrow path upward so I could look down on the bay as the sunlight reflected off the gentle waves.

Interestingly, as I began climbing the steep path, a friendly yellow jacket bee flew alongside me. When I arrived on top and sat to rest on a rock, it flew over and settled on one of the shoulder straps of my backpack just above my heart. I watched, observing it make several short smooth motions. Moments later it flew off so I glanced down to see that it had left a small pile of pollen. I scooped it up by gently brushing my right forefinger along the strap. Touching it to my lips, and then swallowing it, I felt my heart began to expand in spasms, spasms of love. I moved over to lie on a patch of grass where I didn't want to move.

Hummmm...I mused to myself, reflecting. The last time I saw a yellow jacket was while walking the Tor labyrinth in Glastonbury when a similar looking yellow jacket had fallen on the ground sideways and couldn't get up. It was on the 4th level corresponding to the heart. The bee was carrying pollen that must have gotten so heavy that it fell over.

I remembered bending down to turn it over and putting it on my finger so it could get itself reorientated. After a seemingly long minute it flew off. Thus connecting the two experiences, I thought, *Perhaps this little yellow jacket was saying 'thank you' on the part of its relative?*

For our final day, Christy and I went in the direction of the north, when my eyes caught sight of a cloud in an unusual shape hanging over the island of Mull. I slowed down. But Christy, anxious to get to her final beach destination, passed me.

Stopping altogether, I hoped to discern more clearly what exactly was happening. The lenticular shaped cloud had suspended itself above the low mountain on Mull. I opened to my inner vision, my shamanic self, so I could see more precisely, to watch some kind of seemingly extraordinary event happening before my eyes.

White robed beings were in this cloud, possibly inside a ship. I realized they were mysteriously descending into the mountain, almost as if they were stepping down a ladder leading into a large Temple. This Temple had people inside, figures, possibly Priests and/or Priestesses who seemed to be receiving some kind of initiation or teaching.

Suddenly I felt myself be swept up into the center where four golden triangular points met, creating a spinning golden diamond. *I was in it,* wondering if it was happening directly above the Temple or inside it.
Then, seconds or minutes later, I was released and my spinning spirit came back into my body.

Not sure what was happening or how I felt, I found somewhere on the grass to lie down, questioning, *Was this some kind of an initiation and if so, into what?*

I flashed back to my encounter with the being in the white robe outside my balcony in Sedona. He had arrived inside his own diamond shaped vehicle. Now, I too had experienced being in a diamond, but it was a spinning one. A significant moment for me, it was one I wouldn't soon forget.

The following day, I returned to Glastonbury, but Christy went on to London for a plane back to the US. On a Glastonbury street soon after, I ran into a man, a writer I'd met with our group. He knew a lot about Iona's history, so I asked him a few questions about Iona. He mentioned that the island was once referred to as the *Island of the Druids* and had been the primary seat of the *Druid Magi*.

He explained that it was the place where a person became a full Druid Priest or Priestess, after 15 years of an initiatory practice as a *bard* and then 15 more years as an *ovate*. He suggested that my experience had possibly been a *solar initiation. Wow*, I mused, *it was certainly not like any other I'd ever had. What would a 'moon' initiation be like?*

I was staying in a shared house with two others, a man and a woman, friends. Part way up the boat-like hill, known as Wearyall Hill, it was the last house on the left, and just south of the Glastonbury Tor. In fact, this evidently was this same hill where Joseph of Arimathea had arrived two thousand years ago, when his boat ran aground in the marshes.

The story is that he got out wearily, and placed his staff into the ground. Immediately it blossomed and continued to bloom every year since. I was told that cuttings were taken to place in both the Abbey gardens and at the Chalice Well, to activate the sacred memory he had "planted" here.

In the backyard of my temporary house was a garden, but it had not been well tended. Although my room was on the bottom level of the house, built against the hill, the garden area was still a level below it. My sliding glass door opened onto a small terrace, with an expansive view of the distant Glastonbury *Tor*. It was exhilarating having the room placed so auspiciously across from the *Tor,* especially as the full moon was rising just behind it.

Curiously, on my third night, the moon in its fullness hovered over the Tor. I stayed up late reading, but had closed the sliding glass doors to keep out the chilly night air. The curtains were open, however, so I could watch the moon rise.

Suddenly I realized how late it was, midnight, and then I lifted my head, ready to grasp the arms of the chair to stand up and go to bed. "Eeeek!" I screeched and fell back into my chair. Something moved on the porch outside, behind the curtain. I didn't know what to do next. Paralyzed, my heart seemed to skip a few beats. I was being watched. I asked myself, *Do I really want to see what's out there*?

Hesitantly, glancing back over to the curtain, I saw *red frizzy hair sticking out from behind the curtain on the porch.* Someone - something - was hiding there. My heart skipped a few more beats. Immobilized, I was immobilized!

Minutes passed before I got the courage to stand up. When I did, I hoped that whatever or whomever was hiding there would be gone. I turned to grab the doorknob to the hallway, opened it and ran down the hall to find my housemates. The woman gave me a quick dose of rescue remedy to calm me down, while the other, the young man, went outside into the back garden area to see if anything was out there.

He returned, saying he found no traces of any kind of being outside anywhere. In fact they both mentioned that no one staying there had had any encounters like this.

Confused, but calmer, I went back to my room. Sitting down in my chair, I reflected on what had just happened. *Was this another strange encounter with a being from another world?* I admitted that the house was indeed placed right on one of those hollow hills or mounds, possibly with an entrance place into this *otherworld.*

Feeling into my encounter a little more, it seemed that this being was different from myself, but it might in some way be human, though I wasn't sure. I journeyed with my inner vision, where I saw a tall bear-like being with fluffy reddish fur who was holding the hand of a very small bear-like being and they were walking in the garden below my terrace. Then I saw them pass through an entranceway into the hill, going into the earth. *They must live there*, I realized and then understood the situation a little better.

By chance, that next day, I had a meeting scheduled with Kathy Jones, the author and woman who led our group on the "labyrinth walk" around the Glastonbury Tor. As we sat having tea in one of the popular tea shops along Glastonbury's main street, and after I'd described my evening's experience to her, she began relating her story to me:

"I had been called here by these same beings. They would appear in my dreams every full moon, in Wales, where I lived thirty years ago and it was they who called me to Glastonbury."

To her and to many others in Glastonbury, she explained, these Beings were called the *She Bears* or the *Mother's Blessing People.* Furthermore, they were considered the ancient lineage and ancestors of the Feminine.

Kathy then mentioned how unusual my visitation was, because, as far as she knew, I was the first and only person to whom they had ever appeared in their physical form. I felt humbled, bowing my head in reverence to them.

Later, reflecting to myself on Kathy's information I wondered if it had been these *She Bears* that my heart had been 'longing for' each time my tears fell, walking the 4th level of *Tor Labyrinth?* Recognizing that my intention at the beginning was *to connect with and know better our ancient feminine roots, lineages and ancestors,* I accepted that I had called them to me. It was indeed an honor and showed me how strong the force behind an intention can be. Clearly my quest to know the lineage of the ancient feminine ancestors had officially begun.

Chapter 10 – The Priestess

*S*he was calling to me now to come closer to her, to find my ancient feminine roots, closed down for hundreds, maybe thousands of years.
My Glastonbury pilgrimage had been a good beginning. Now I was waiting to embrace a new perspective about the feminine spirit, the *Priestess* and the great goddess who stood behind her. I was ready to experience her in a more tangible way.

Robert was supportive of my new focus on the feminine, the priestess. Returning from Glastonbury, I was happy to see him and shared my stories. In fact, he liked hearing about the spinning diamond in Iona and about the *She Bears* visiting me, especially because he worked so closely with these realms. Curious to know more, he began looking into the feminine stories and archetypes in his own quiet moments, he soon confessed.

Looking for someone to guide me in my new focus, I quickly learned about a woman from Tucson, Nicole Christine, who had created a nine-month process, called *Awakening the Priestess Within*. I was curious. It hadn't been introduced into Sedona yet, but I learned that there would be a group beginning in the fall of 1995 in Flagstaff, so, without hesitation, I signed up.

The word *Priestess*, however, honestly, was a new word for me, one that I never recognized as being a part of my daily life. Although I read about her in ancient histories of the British Isles, Greece, Egypt and even

Rome, I hadn't experienced who exactly she was, or how she might have any long-term effect on my life.

Then I found in *Priestess of Avalon, Priestess of the Goddess,* where Kathy Jones, my new acquaintance from Avalon, wrote:

"The word 'Priestess' speaks to that part of ourselves…that longs to bring meaning back into mundane life, that thirsts for a true spirituality which is directly connected to the land on which we live or have lived…. in other lives, when we were aligned with the Goddess, as the Source of all that is. She stands for the ancient forgotten virtues, the powers of women and the celebration of our mysteries, of hidden knowledge… holiness… enchantment and revelation." [2]

Thus, by participating in the *Awakening the Priestess Within,* I anticipated being given an invitation to discern and reclaim my whole story, the one that went back to these ancient feminine roots, which had never changed. And it was not just me, I felt like these roots must be at the heart of every woman.

In this process we would be meeting one full day during a weekend of each month and then an extended evening. It was designed to support myself and the other initiates to delve deeply into our psyches, so we could access the suppressed priestess consciousness.

We touched on what the priestess had represented in the past, before her spirit and spiritual life had been so successfully subdued when the temples were closed and the patriarch with its different life principals took control.

In fact Aleia, our facilitator read us an early flashback Nicole wrote, describing her memory of running with a group of priestesses in these ancient times:

"We were running through an underground tunnel carrying scrolls under our arms. Invaders hostile to the teachings of the Goddess were destroying the Temple, and we were fleeing with as many recorded mysteries as we each could carry. As we ran, we vowed that the teachings would not be lost and alchemically encoded the contents of each scroll we carried into our genetic codes to be brought forth, when it was again safe for the Goddess to return. We had not known how many, many, many lifetimes we would have to reincarnate in one disguise after another, before we could come forward again as priestesses and live the teachings, live the Great Mysteries. And that time is now! At last, that time is now!"

After hearing this I wanted to know more about the matriarchal consciousness, what it had been like and how it changed when the patriarch took over, what specifically was lost. We discussed how the matrilineal culture had once been a cohesive culture focused on honoring the sacredness of the earth and the waters. It was when the priestess was the mediator between the world of the divine and that of humans, before it changed to a world of power, force and militarization when men took it over.

My heart warmed as I tried to imagine this matrilineal society, when priestesses' lives focused on fertility and abundance, realizing that caretaking the sacred places of the goddess was also because she was the one who granted them abundance. Moreover it made fertility the core of their existence. I knew there was much more to understand, to remember.

Curious to grasp a concept of what I had lost, to know what exactly I was hoping to reclaim, I knew it was still probably deep in my subconscious. It had been such a long time, thousands of years.

Our sessions were intimate, safe. It felt that our group was like a pod of dolphins, as we processed first our individual emotions and aspirations, before what they were together in a bigger picture. Surrendering to the process I became vulnerable. Because I never felt safe in my early life, my mother being unpredictable, our Flagstaff facilitator, Aleia, provided a supportive container for the inner work. It invited me to be more present in each moment, more grounded.

Our second session was an important core piece for me as a ceremony was offered for each of us to reclaim our young maiden selves, no matter what our age. It would take us each back to when we had our first period, our first blood, which symbolized us stepping into our womanhood.

Evidently this ceremony was once part of an ancient priestess tradition of honoring a girl when she became a woman, which also embraced her sexuality. Unfortunately it is not a part of our society today, as neither our mothers nor the female community seem to celebrate this significance. In fact it has been a long time, hundreds of years, maybe thousands, since it has been, I imagined.

Furthermore, I remembered wanting to hide when I was bleeding, and sometimes referred to my period as "the curse". Now I was realizing that stepping through this doorway was not only about the physical level of becoming a woman but also about the spiritual level.

Living in Arizona and being surrounded by Native American tribes, I soon learned that they do still honor a girl when she becomes a woman. The Hopi, Navajo and Apaches do. In fact they celebrate it with a ceremony that can last for days, as with the Apaches. They recognize when a girl has her first blood; it signifies, not only that she has the potential to carry life as a woman, but that she is considered and honored as a 'vision holder' for the tribe. She is invited to take her place beside the older, wise women.

During our ceremony each woman was invited to have a turn sitting in a beautifully decorated chair with flowers, as her priestess sisters surrounded her. We offered her gifts, massaged her feet, combed her hair and did anything to make her feel special, which included speaking loving words of support.

When it was my turn, I moved over and sat in the chair. One initiate, spontaneously moved over in front of me and handed me a bright pink rose, saying, "This rose brings the gift of love to you as it is time to accept your beauty within," and then another sister began massaging my feet while still another brushed my hair softly the way I would love to have had my mother do for a special moment like this.

Aleia, the process facilitator came over and crouched in front of me, carrying a small vile of an essential oil, rose and put some on my forehead then on my heart, saying, "You are so honored and adored by the great mother. She is with you in every moment watching and supporting you as you reclaim and walk again on this timeless path."

I couldn't hide my tears as they flowed from my eyes, streaming down my cheeks. There were no words to describe my feelings. Moments passed before I stood up, bowed my head, declaring to my new sisters, *This moment will stay with me always, I thank you all for this beautiful honoring.* I stepped away from the chair leaving it for the next woman. I felt valued and loved, respected as a 'new' woman no matter what my age.

During another session a few months later, we were invited to write our spiritual story, the one that led us to the present moment in our lives. Slipping back into my past to write about it, then reading it out loud, my sisters listening, it opened me up. Not only was I being seen, aspects of my story were being heard for the first time. This exercise marked a significant rite of passage for me that once completed, allowed me to let the past go, in anticipation of my new story.

Weeks before the priestess process began, Robert and I moved to a small house in the West Sedona area under Thunder Mountain, the most visible mountain because it is in the center of Sedona. Also, it was within walking distance from our house.

Most every afternoon I walked up to sit at the foot of this mountain, to meditate near a tall thin red rock spire set high above me. It appeared to have one eye looking out at me.

One day I began having a conversation with this rock being who seemed to be a female and to whom I began referring as Isis after the famous Egyptian Goddess. She began telling me things, supporting me while I was in the *Awakening the Priestess Within*. In fact, weeks before my ordination ceremony I went to meditate with her and she gave me an image of the dress she suggested I make with the exact color.

Emphatic, she also described the pearl crown-like headpiece she wanted me to wear with a purple amethyst crystal hanging from it over my third eye. When the moment arrived I did make this ceremonial outfit, exactly as she had suggested. It was with the help of friend, as it was the first dress I'd ever made.

While in the middle of my Priestess Process I thought to invite Lady Olivia Robertson to Sedona for her first visit to Arizona when I learned that she traveled to the US each year because other *Fellowship of Isis* affiliates in California and other states wanted her participation in ceremonies they did. She came all the way from her castle home in Ireland.

The *Fellowship of Isis* had been founded by Lady Olivia Robertson and her brother the Baron and Rev. Lawrence Durdin-Robertson, in 1976. They claimed connection to and were evidently part of a priestly line that came to them through their hereditary relationship to the Egyptian Princess, Scota, thought to be the daughter of Isis.

Through their family priesthood, the ceremony of "Ordination" was offered with no vows required or commitments to secrecy. Thus, our priestess process was associated with the *Fellowship of Isis*, and linked directly to the well-known Priestess and Egyptian Goddess, Isis.

Interestingly, Lady Olivia was in her early eighties when she made her first visit to Arizona. She was as spunky and enthusiastic as any 30 year old, offering limitless wisdom and knowledge to all of us who crossed her path.

In fact I remember the ceremony we did with her in Flagstaff. All the priestesses from earlier groups in Flagstaff were invited to participate. We gathered in a large community room with our hands joined in a circle when Lady Olivia called in Isis.

My mouth dropped open in disbelief when I felt hundreds of white wings suddenly surround us. It felt like I had been transported through some dimensional portal inside a temple, somewhere lost in time. It was magnificent.

Then Lady Olivia came down to Sedona for a day allowing me to show her some of the famous areas she'd already read about. In a few places she insisted on anchoring Isis through me: Bell Rock, the Chapel Area and then under Thunder Mountain. She repeated often in her distinct English accent, "I love how these red rocks engage my senses, this desert area. It's so different from my home in Ireland where I am always surrounded by the green hills." I knew she would return in a year and we would have more experiences together.

However, before the nine month *Awakening the Priestess Within* process had concluded, I was inspired to organize a trip, a pilgrimage, to southern France so priestesses could connect to the places of Mary Magdalene there. I had an affinity for France having already lived there for several years. But when a friend I'd met on the Glastonbury trip told me about this certain area, it got my attention. I wanted to know more.

Chapter 11 – Holy Blood, Holy Grail and France

During my Glastonbury journey in 1995 a woman called Alena who did a past life regression for our group, told us about a controversial book called *Holy Blood, Holy Grail* after we had seen a private theatrical presentation about Mary Magdalene. The play had initiated discussions about who she really was, her true story.

Alena and I continued talking about France, because she'd lived in the mysterious area for eleven years where much of the book focused. She said it told about a small village, *Rennes Le Chateau,* located in the southwestern part of France and that it spoke about Magdalene's coming to France for safety after the crucifixion.

France was a familiar place for me because I'd already spent years there as a photographer documenting the lives of the French peasant farmers, although not the area mentioned in the book. Thus I knew the language.

Published in 1982 she told me that the book presented such shocking information it gained immediate worldwide attention. Addressing myths the Catholic Church created long ago it became the first major book to suggest the truth about Mary Magdalene's identity, with details about her being the wife of Jesus and mother of his children. Furthermore, it proposed that Jesus did not die on the cross.

I could see that the Catholic Church would not want these stories told, as any of them could destroy foundational beliefs it had fabricated and maintained for so long.

The book was written by three well-respected English journalists and researchers, Henry Lincoln, Michael Baigent and Richard Leigh and Alena said that it talked about not only the true teachings of Jesus but his mysterious lineage.

Evidently the information written about Mary Magdalene invited people to find the truth about who Magdalene really was, her lost legacies. The book got my attention not only because it touch on the lost identity of Mary Magdalene, but because it could touch my own lost feminine spirit. In fact Mary Magdalene seemed to be representing all women, including priestesses, whose lineages and legacies had been hidden for thousands of years.

With my affinity for France, the idea came to me about creating a sacred journey that could be a life changing experience for participants. Not only would they walk in places Mary Magdalene had left her legacy it might also be about reclaiming symbolically a part of themselves that had been lost.

I suspected that my friend Alena knew of many hidden places in the land there and that she too probably guarded many secrets, from when she had lived there for eleven years. Thus, several months later after I'd returned to Sedona and read the book, *Holy Blood, Holy Grail*, I asked her to design a journey for a group in the late spring. I would bring the people.

The book gave me many details about the mystery of the village Alena mentioned, Rennes Le Chateau, with its church and special tower. It told about the church that *Abbe Sauniere*, the parish priest at the turn of the century was renovating when he mysteriously discovered coded documents in one of the pillars beneath the altar. Evidently, after immediately taking them to Paris he returned a rich man. They must of have carried information of great significance.

The source of his money has always been a mystery, but he used it to build the *Tour Magdala* and to renovate the church. Then he dedicated both to Mary Magdalene.

Whatever Sauniere discovered written in those documents it became an enigma that has become one of the more famous around the world. Personally, I suspected that these secret documents might contain information about Jesus' marriage to Mary Magdalene, but that is just my theory.

Alena mentioned that after numerous books had been written about Rennes Le Chateau people still questioned what was hidden beneath the mystical hill. In fact, she said that since the book's publication tens of thousands of people have felt called to southern France, to Rennes Le Chateau, to explore these many legends in hopes of grasping truth for themselves.

Not only coming to explore stories about Mary Magdalene and Jesus, they also were coming to learn more about the ancient Order of Knights Templar and the famous Cathars whose stories were entwined within the mysteries of the Rennes Le Chateau area. Curiously, they had both been persecuted by the Catholic Church.

After I researched more, it seemed that both the Knights Templar and the Cathars had achieved a power or wisdom that the church wanted to suppress. The Cathar had their beliefs, their gnosis that were possibly connected with the Essene beliefs of being independently connected with God without the necessity of an intermediary like the Catholic Church. They lived close to the land doing their initiations in caves where nothing could disturb them.

The Knights Templar were a medieval warrior-monk type order whose history was more elusive. I read that not only did they have secret treasures, but interestingly were said to be protectors of the true lineage and bloodline of Jesus. Furthermore, they must have known the truth about his marriage and children with Mary Magdalene.

They had also become a wealthy order from properties the joining members surrendered to them, when they took vows of poverty and obedience. Thus it was the French King who coveted these properties and their new prestige and called on the Catholic Church to denounce any support of the Templars, which they did. Originally the Pope had supported the Templars as a sovereign order, when they protected the pilgrimage routes to the Holy Land taken by thousands of people.

Thus, the Rennes Le Chateau area with all its mysteries was where I would be bringing the first group with my friend Alena. Having so many places to experience in connection with its hidden past, this trip could offer each participant the adventure of a lifetime.

After much organization, I had a group of women mostly from Arizona who either had done a nine month Priestess training or who were in the process, like myself. Nicole helped inspire some women to join the trip, because she too would participate. It would be her first quest into the Magdalene mysteries of southern France.

Chapter 12 – France - The Journey Begins

Turning off the highway from the Toulouse airport onto a smaller road, we headed in the direction of Rennes Le Chateau. It was mid May 1996. Alena and her husband Jay had picked me up at the airport, as I came early. I was with my new friend Ann who I'd met on the Glastonbury trip.

Alena was a slender woman with shoulder length curly brown hair and a broad inspiring smile. Jay was a charismatically handsome surfer from Australia having the English accent but pronouncing it with a different inflection. He would be driving the van for our group.

Touching my feet down in France again after so many years was opening my heart. I admired the beauty of the tall white sycamore trees lining the many roadways, the luscious green pastures dotted with cows and their young calves grazing in the distance and of the endless rows of twisted well-tended grape vines growing in so many fields. It was welcoming.

I began to flash on my earlier experiences as a photographer when I was documenting the last French peasants, farming traditionally with their oxen before technology took over. It was a time when men and women worked together caring for mother earth, who returned their care with an abundant harvest. It was a basic, simple life they had. My being part of it, witnessing it, changed my life then. And now, on a different quest, more specifically tilling up deeper aspects of my own feminine mysteries, it felt like my life might change again.

As we drove into a landscape where mountains appeared in the distance, Jay pointed to them showing, "Over there you see the foothills of the Pyrenees that sit between France and Spain," as my eyes followed his finger.

Narrowing, the road followed the Aude River where pale colored grasses blew in the wind on the hills above, after which Alena pointed out the famous village of Rennes Le Chateau on a distant hilltop. Then we arrived in a tiny town called Couiza at the foot of Rennes Le Chateau where we crossed an arched bridge and headed to another destination.

While crossing this short bridge, I glanced up at a high mountain to the left, called Pech Cardou and then quickly up to the right, where I saw a high castle ruin, *Chateau Blanchfort*, Alena told us. It seemed to create the other side of some kind of unseen doorway through which we were about to pass. Slowly we drove between these ancient places like we were being birthed into what I would soon find to be the famous thermal waters of Rennes Les Bains.

As soon as we passed stone bath house ruins Alena said were from the turn of the century, she added that the special thermal waters were what brought the Romans here more than two thousand years ago.

Then we arrived in the tiny town of Rennes Les Bains (the Baths of the Queen) where Ann and I were going to be left for three days while Alena and Jay made some final arrangements for our group. Luckily, I spoke French.

In front of L'Hotel de France, the only hotel in the village, Jay stopped the van so we could get out. Gathering our suitcases and minimal belongings, we nodded goodbye as they assured us they'd be back to pick us up. I felt at the mercy of this unknown place as they drove off.

We looked at each other, Ann and I, before walking through the heavy French wooden doors into the hotel where we were met face to face with the proprietor. She was a short slender woman in her late forties.

Probably at least 100 years old, the hotel had mustiness about it. Not the dust particles lingering within the wall's creases, but the ancient energies that felt like they had been left here from a long passed era. I realized that it might be from thousands of years ago, after I learned that first the Celts and later the Romans had lived here.

When the proprietor went into her office to check the reservations and find us rooms, I strolled down the dark hallway. On the opposite wall to her office hung a very large painting. In it, something had caused people to collapse on the streets, where a tall obelisk looking object had toppled over. It seemed that someone had also been beheaded, or no, it was a statue that had fallen over and the head had rolled in another direction. *What was this force that caused people to be collapsing in the streets*, I wondered, questioning why such a painting would be hung in this hotel.

The proprietor popped out of her office ready to walk us to our rooms. Mounting the stairs to the second floor we were both given rooms with balconies overlooking the Sals River. Ann's room was red, with one big bed and mine was blue with twin beds. It seemed like a perfect beginning. We sanctioned ourselves to our rooms for a moment. I lifted my suitcase onto the second bed, soon ready to step out on the balcony to the soothing sounds of the river. I sat on one of the folding chairs and knew sleep would come easy here.

Then Ann came out on her balcony and we laughed together joking about how we were creating our new neighborhood. Time passed before we decided to march down the carpeted stairs and have dinner in the hotel's sparsely seated dining room. Food would be a wonderful welcome in this unfamiliar place.

It was a good French dinner after which I finished with my favorite crème brulee desert, a custard with the sugar broiled to a crispiness on top. After we climbed the stairs to our rooms. I was ready to retire early. In fact I was in bed with the lights out within an hour after dinner.

Then it began. As if the curtains had been pulled back for an after dinner movie playing on a full screen it was *showtime*. But my eyes were closed tight. I was being catapulted into some kind of lucid dream that couldn't be delayed another minute. The screen displayed images that began coming fast, one right after another as if they were previews of coming events.

The images began with an equal armed cross that morphed into a four-pointed star and came right at me and hovered. Then, I saw what looked like two tablets lying side by side, with distinct writing on them, but I couldn't make it out and didn't try. They were placed on the top of something rectangular, heavy.

Next, I saw a Being, standing, who appeared to be wearing what looked like meshed, wire-type armor like I had never seen before. He stood against an earthen embankment, down a passageway in the earth where he seemed to be guarding a doorway.

Then a white-haired man in a white robe came out to greet me from either a dark tunnel or a low curved archway. Curiously, in the same moment my ring mysteriously slid off the finger of my left hand. Aware of it happening, I seemed to be watching from a different reality, or timeline. (I found it the next morning in my bed). Then the movie was over or my awareness of it was over as I fell into a deep sleep.

Our breakfast the next morning offered a choice of small French baguettes, croissants and pain au chocolate (a bread with chocolate inside). And there was also fruit, tea and coffee. I was a tea drinker but Ann savored the famous French coffee. As we each put these luscious breads into our longing mouths we each declared the desire would soon stop.

During breakfast, I told Ann about my movie-like experiences the night before. She listened, but declared her sleep had been undisturbed. Finally satiated, we got up from our table and stepped out beyond the French doors for our first Rennes Les Bains experience. We walked over to stand on the bridge next to the hotel, which arched over the fast moving river and stood there side by side looking in both directions.

Below us and slightly upstream, we saw Le Bain Fort, the hot bath, where waters flowing from a hole in the stone wall next to it, was continuously filling the tub. One person was lying down while others dipped their feet in it from opposite ends. We watched several people, each taking a turn, when Ann and I proclaimed to each other that as the day warmed up, we too would venture into these hot waters.

We continued to the other side of the bridge and turned beside a row of old stone houses built against the hill. Before the last house, we took a path to the left, marked by a small square sign saying it was an old Roman road. Stones had been laid unevenly on the ground as we followed to a tiny footbridge under which water flowed from somewhere above us.

Crossing to an area of grass overlooking the waters, we found a spot to sit near one another. Ann giggled a little saying, "Oops I just sat on a patch of wet leaves," and got up to move over, wiping her jeans. I laughed at her, exclaiming, "Yes and you never know what might be hiding under them, fairies or other surprises of an unknown kind." She laughed before we each got settled.

Sounds of the water played in my ears like a soothing symphony as I slipped into my other vision. Again images continued appearing before me. I sensed an arch that was forming over the waters below me where there was a small pool of water and then another arch appeared crossing it.

Lost in this other world I suddenly sensed that Ann had stood up so I opened my eyes. "I want to return to the hotel and change my wet pants," she said. "OK, I think I'll stay," I replied. "We can meet up later. " Then I moved down to sit closer to the pool of water on a small beach-like area.

Continuing in my vision, I mysteriously saw a circular room where the tablets I'd seen the night before were laid on top of a rectangular box. At four areas of the room beings in white robes stood guarding it before four angels came down and joined them. Fascinated, I saw the rounded ceiling of this room appearing earthen-like and that it could open to the outside world when something caused it to do so.

But then the man with the white hair, St. Germain he said, the one who appeared the night before, returned because he wanted to take me into this room. Although I was in this other world I could still feel the energy. It was so strong my stomach felt excruciating pain.

He held a wand-like instrument in his hand with which he moved around the tablets clockwise three times, magically helping my stomach to feel better. Too soon however the curtains came down and this scene was over.

Early the next day I made a trip back to find my spot on the beach area next to the little pond to meditate. Deep in stillness I enjoyed a new strength and energy I soon felt inside. Reviewing the circumstances I wondered if maybe the *tablets* that were being displayed before me could possibly be from the *Arc of the Covenant?*

I flashed on the painting hanging in the hotel hallway whereby everyone in it was passed out on the ground seemingly from some kind of overwhelming influence. I'd heard about the effects the *Arc* could have on people nearby it, if they were not in the right consciousness. In fact I remembered reading that the guardian/keepers of the *Arc* wore special stones on a breastplate to protect themselves.

Hearing some kind of splashing noise nearby, I quickly opened my eyes. Lying directly in front of me was an asp-like snake half in the water attempting to swallow a large worm. I watched as it swayed its head back and forth trying to swallow it when finally it succeeded.

I smoothly got up and stepped back knowing it was a poisonous snake. It tried to swim upstream, to no avail, as the little eddy was too strong for it. Finally it surrendered and was carried back by the eddy. I squatted down as it swam in front of me to the other side where it finally seemed content.

Remembering brief details about the *Arc of the Covenant,* I knew that the asps were somehow related to it. Thus having this snake appear might be affirming a truth of my vision. Possibly the arc had passed here or maybe something about it had been left in another timeline here, in another dimension. I had never experienced having a vision like this.

Since so much had been revealed to me from other worlds in this ancient town, after only three days. I wondered what would happen next. Early the next morning Alena and Jay picked us up in front of L'Hotel de France, as we had arranged. We would drive to meet the group arriving in Toulouse. I was ready for our eleven day "pilgrimage" to begin.

Chapter 13 – Priestesses in France

Eager to experience the famous land of the Magdalene, the group was waiting together at the Toulouse airport when we arrived. It was a gathering of the "sisterhood" in France and our first journey together outside of Arizona.

There were women from Tucson I was meeting for the first time, but the three women from Flagstaff and the two from California I already knew from the Glastonbury trip. Most had done the "Awakening the Priestess Within" process except the California women. And I had two more sessions to go before completing my process to "emerge," after my Ordination.

Ann had brought along a beautiful Hawaiian CD, *The Calling,* of soft rhythmic chants with whale sounds in the background. Jay played it in the van as we drove from the airport. Some of the women made spontaneous dance moves while sitting side by side.

When we turned off the main highway, it was already late afternoon as the van climbed a narrow paved road lined with tall poplar trees escorting us to the door of our B&B. Just before arriving however, the road passed fields of purple lavender whose scents engaged my senses pleasantly.

Of old stone, the B&B was on two levels. Jay left the van below in the parking area as I gathered my suitcase and climbed the outer stairs to the front door with the other women. We drew straws to see who would be together in the shared rooms. My roommate was a Flagstaff friend Merion we soon discovered after holding up our same colored straws. Our beds were near the spacious living room where the group would gather each morning.

Our personal chef was preparing a welcome dinner to introduce us to the sensuous French cuisine. In fact he would be cooking for many of our meals, Alena informed us.

That first evening after our welcome dinner, most women said they were tired from the long flights, and ready for bed. But then Jay put *The Calling* on the CD player, and suddenly several perked up and started to move their bodies. Backwards, forwards, up and down, softly they carried the gentle swing of the Hawaiian waves with them as they glided off to bed.

The following morning we came down to have our French traditional breakfast of delicate and addictive breads served with the infamous French coffee. We also had fruit, yogurt and cereal, as the chef knew Americans ate differently.

In the living room afterword, each woman expressed her intention for joining this ten-day journey. Equally, we hoped the mysteries hidden in this ancient land might deepen the connection to our lost feminine roots. I knew that I hoped it would unveil new aspects of my evolving priestess self.

Alena explained that she would be taking us on a journey each day to special places but would only give us a brief summary of each. "I will keep the details for later; if you hear too much about a place, before, it can overshadow your first experience."

The first day Jay drove us up the winding road to the top of Rennes Le Chateau. The journey up moved us from one side to the other of the van's three rows of bench-like seats, back and forth, as we climbed higher. Some women chatted and pointed at the landscape views and to the ruins of an old Cathar castle on a distant hill. But I was quiet, feeling this was an important moment for me, as we drove closer.

Suddenly, just before arriving at the top, I started seeing streams of light pouring out of the hill. It was like four pillars were shooting up from beneath the village. I tried to discern specifically what I was seeing, questioning, *Where these pillars of light coming out from some kind of hidden temple here?* But then the vision stopped.

As Jay swerved the van out of the last hair-raising curve, so close to the edge that dropped straight down, I muffled a scream. But then we entered the village. Only one car could pass at a time.

Immediately on our right I saw an old castle. Seemingly run down it had two high towers one rounded, the other square. Eeriness surrounded this castle as if it had appeared from another period and was still hung with fragments of lost time, each carrying a small part of a larger mystery. Would you dare open the door and step into it? Not me.

Alena referred to it as a "Merovingian" castle, which had housed the last royal noble family who lived here in the late 1700s, the Hautpouls. She told us that the woman Marie de Negre d'Ables, the Dame d'Hautpoul-Blanchefort was the last person who died here in 1781. Buried in the graveyard behind the Magdalene Church, she was also the last to be carrying some great secret that is still a mystery today Alena informed us.

After we passed this sandstone castle, other low buildings appeared on the same side the street including what were once the stables which housed horses used by those living in this castle. Then I saw a building of the same light colored stone on the opposite side with a small garden next to it. A short gray haired woman quickly popped out of her house wearing the traditional French country-style apron over her skirt and sweater. She stepped into her garden with high rubber boots and stood in the moist soil bending over as if she were planting something.

Truthfully I thought she wanted to know who was in this large white van moving slowly past her door. She squinted her eyes and kept her gaze directly on our van as we passed. But then the road made a sharp left curve to a higher place, where Jay parked the van.

Mesmerized by the landscape view below I stepped out to face the distant mountains. Rennes Le Chateau sat high in this landscape and I realized it held a unique position above what was happening far below. It must have been important in past times.

Turning my gaze to the right I saw an unusual square structure of stone with a rounded high tower. It protruded over the edge of the hill with a cutout square design on the top. It was the *Tour Magdala,* Alena told us.

Then she quickly whisked us off down to the Magdalene church hoping to take us inside. But when she arrived at the door, it was shut tight, barred. In shock Alena bolted over to the next building, the museum, to find out why. She found out that someone had entered the church earlier that morning and cut off the head of the crouching, slightly stooped sculpted figure, *Asmodeus,* who greeted people at the door. Nothing this bizarre had ever happened in Rennes Le Chateau. Thus, in disbelief, the people closed the church doors so they could decide what to do.

Meanwhile we were escorted over to the *Tour Magdala,* the building jutting out with the rounded tower I'd seen earlier. We climbed the steps to the curved esplanade that stretched around and overlooked the valley below. The *Tour Magdala* was at one end of it while an open glass structure was at the other where birds and flowers had once been kept, Alena told us.

First entering the lower room of the Tour we climbed the tight spiral of twenty-two steps to the top, where a heavy door opened onto the tower area. It showed breathtaking landscape views in every direction, 360 degrees.

This was the tower the famous Rennes Le Chateau priest, Abbe Sauniere had built with the mysterious monies from his church renovation discovery in the 1890s. Alena informed us that he made the lower room into his library and put his books and desk there.

First she stood in the direction of the east, on the stone bench, with her left hand pointing. "We have an ancient landscape temple here in the shape of a pentagram and here are two of its special points. That one over there ", as she pointed to a volcanic mountain, "is the one they call Mt. Bugarach and holds many mysteries, including ones of early Essene groups and of the Cathars. It is also near where Jules Verne lived when he wrote, *Journey To The Center of The Earth*."

Turning slightly to the south, she continued, "That one over there is where a Templar headquarters was located called *Bezu.* " I could only identify a high peak but it was difficult to see anything on it. "But this long ridge," as her finger traced a line of limestone that extended out into the landscape below Bezu, "leads to the center point of the five pointed star, called La Pique. And the valley below it is called, *La Valdieu,* The Valley of God."

I took a moment to absorb her valuable information storing it in my own inner library as I moved around the Tour/tower area. Then she added, "And Rennes Le Chateau is also situated on one of the pentagram points."

Alena mentioned that she once lived near La Valdieu for about eight years during her time in the area. However she never mentioned that the "holy family" which probably included Mary Magdalene and Jesus (possibly their daughter Sarah), were known to have passed through this area and possibly lived near La Valdieu. It was years later before I learned about this.

As we descended the Tour Magdala's twisting staircase to the esplanade, we walked to the glass structure at the other end, looked out and then took the steps down to the ground level. They also numbered 22. Interestingly there were 22 steps going up and then 22 going down.

"Does that mean something?" I asked her. "Yes," she answered, "perhaps it is identifying two different realities, the seen and the unseen, the real and illusionary worlds." Frustrated, I wanted to know what this was all about here, the bigger story.

Exploring the church and graveyard had to wait for another day. We left the tiny village down the Rennes Le Chateau road, but then Jay turned onto a pale grassy farm road that swung around beneath the Tour Magdala. I wondered why they were taking us along this barely visible path into the lower field. No sooner had Jay put on the music, *The Calling* when we all screamed for him to stop the van so we could get out and dance in this mystical landscape.

Faster than I could have ever imagined we were suddenly moving our bodies to this evocative aloha music below Rennes Le Chateau. I felt free, expanded, happily creating new body movements. Then Alena and Jay came together to dance. She was a very theatrical person possibly having once been on stage as an actress or a singer for a group. Then we learned that she met

Jay here at Rennes Le Chateau years earlier when they both lived here.

Intertwining her body with his she moved erotically with him as we all moved over to surround them. We each continued to dance our own rhythms with the music, when Alena culminated her final movement by twisting her leg around his just as the music stopped.

Fascinated, I felt that this dance brought us into oneness, like it had actually been some ancient ritual. As if we had been performing before an audience, it would have been one consisting of visitors exploring the mysteries of the Tour Magdala, who, after glancing down at the landscape below the Tour, might have spotted us and began to watch.

They probably thought it intriguing, a group of women dancing to Hawaiian music blasting from a van. All the while they probably questioned what it really was we were so passionately exploring that might be hidden deep in the Earth below us.

A few days later Alena led us through a past life regression. It was to give us a more personal connection not only to ourselves, but to a possible memory from an earlier lifetime here. My regression took me back to a lifetime whereby I saw a white tower-like building deep in the ground, possibly the very field below the Tour Magdala. It was clean, old, maybe from *Atlantis*, where I found myself in a special room wearing a pale yellow robe.

My hair was very long, reddish brown in color and I carried a wand. I was standing around what seemed to be something in the center of this room like a large pale yellow crystal. I saw myself as the caretaker of this crystal and would walk around it, sometimes looking up at it, as if it were situated above me. In this session I saw myself working with other women, Priestesses.

Each woman wore a long robe, but mine was the only yellow one. Our mission as Priestesses was to be in the highest purest vibration of love as we stood in a circle around the center, the Crystal. We then "fed" our pure heart energy into the Crystal after which the earthen ceiling of the room opened up. The crystal would shoot up its strong pale yellow light into the heavens to connect with companion planets and stars keeping them aligned with the Earth.

At the end of this lifetime I passed the wand to a younger woman, a Priestess who would be the next caretaker of the Crystal. This was the life of the Sisterhood here, a simple life without feelings of loneliness. Thus caretaking this Crystal was my work, our work together.

After coming out of the regression I felt a twinge in my heart. Probably the session helped me feel a deeper connection to my Priestess self and I began realizing why visions of remembering these ancient things were being revealed to me so fast.

The following day the church was open. The missing head had been quickly recreated and put back on the figure so it was ready to greet people who entered the church.

Again we climbed the winding road to the village, the same sharp curves but I noticed myself calmer. At the top we left our van and walked toward the Tour Magdala, then down to the Magdalene church.

As soon as I stepped inside the open wooden doors of the church a figure was glaring at me. Flashes of white were coming from its wild looking eyes above its distortedly angled mouth. It was crouched to my left. Two pointed horns were on its head; but when I looked down I saw it had claw-like fingers. It was *Asmodeus,* the figure beheaded just the day before. I thought it a curious place to put a statue of something people refer to as the *Devil*.

My religious upbringing was not Catholic, thus going into Catholic churches was not a norm for me. However I knew this figure was not found in Catholic Churches. I soon learned that to explore the hidden mysteries of Mary Magdalene and Jesus coming here, it included researching inside specific churches, Catholic ones. Secrets were being passed down in them.

Sometimes they were found in stained glass windows or certain gestures such as the hand or knee stance of a statue, I was quickly learning from Alexis. Or they could be found in the placement of certain objects in the churches camouflaged from the scrutiny of the Catholic Church.

My father disliked the Catholic Church emphatically, coming from a Scottish and English background. Thus we children were raised as Protestants, or more correctly, as Christian Scientists where there was a father/mother god belief. We learned how some beliefs and ways of looking at the world were just illusions. Moreover, the philosophy or theology made me strong in many ways and I recognized later that it was probably the "New Age" church of its time.

Paradoxically now, I was being challenged to step into these dwellings, the entanglement from which my father had hoped to distance us. Quickly having to acclimate myself, I would be stepping into endless numbers of churches in the next years to purposely pick up a detail here and there about the hidden story of Mary Magdalene, Jesus and their lineage in France.

Thus, walking down the aisle in the Magdalene church with its long wooden benches on each side, I looked for a good place to sit. I found a bench near the altar where the others were already seated. Under the arched ceiling painted pale blue with gold stars everywhere were two obvious figures. One on the right, the other on the left, each was holding a baby. The figures were Mary and Joseph who we all thought had had one "holy child." Now Alena was addressing the mystery shown here that Jesus had a twin.

I was shocked. A few other women were also visibly in shock, as we then listened carefully when she pointed out the fourteen Stations of the Cross surrounding us on the church walls. She pointed to this last station saying, "In this last one, do you see a moon clearly shining?" We all looked over at it. "Well," she continued, "do you see those two men taking Jesus off the cross?" We all nodded. "Well in Jewish tradition a dead body was never touched after sunset, so this scene is showing that Jesus must not have been dead when they took him down. It is after sunset."

Thus Jesus had not died on the cross and Abbe Sauniere had placed this truth out in the open for all to see if they wanted to accept it. I sat quietly letting these possibilities find a place in my old thought patterns.

Then I glanced down at the lower part of the altar on which Sauniere had painted a scene with Magdalene kneeling on the ground with a skull next to her. It appeared that she was outside of a 'grotto' or cave, with her hands on her lap as she glanced into this cave at something not shown. There was an open book beside her. I learned years later that when a book was open like this, it symbolized that certain knowledge was known. In this case it probably related to what was being intimated here, that something important might be hidden in a nearby cave. Maybe it was a body? Who might it be?

The energy of the church was strong, peaceful where I was sitting but when I got up and walked down the aisle to exit I felt density, discomfort. A statue of

Magdalene was halfway down on my left holding her sacred jar I presumed was filled with anointing oil. Next to her stood a tall thin wooden cross. We were informed that because the bark was still on it, it was still living, evidently another clue that Jesus had not died on the cross.

Approaching the door to leave, I noticed the baptismal water placed above Asmodeus on my right side. I gazed up higher to four angelic figures in pale robes of blue and gold looking down. They were depicted crossing themselves as one would when entering a Catholic Church, but the statement written in gold letters underneath them was in Latin. Alexis translated it as, "By this symbol, I will conquer *him.*"

Who is him? I wondered. Normally one might think that it was directed at the devil, Asmodeus, referring to beliefs the Catholic Church had fabricated about good and evil. Later, I found that there were other scenarios of who Asmodeus might be.

Researching, I discovered that he was known as the guardian of the doorway to the Temple of Solomon in Jerusalem. Curious, why had Sauniere placed him here as a guardian, I asked myself? What might he be guarding?

I flashed back to when we arrived on this France journey and Alena had placed a welcoming postcard on everyone's pillow with a photo of Rennes Le Chateau. On it she wrote, *Welcome to the New Temple Of Jerusalem.* Perhaps she was giving us a hint that maybe Rennes Le Chateau held powerful secrets affiliated with those in Solomon's Temple at the heart of Jerusalem.

What could be hidden here that was also inside Soloman's Temple? Could it be the *Arc of The Covenant,* or something else I wondered? Suddenly overwhelmed, hearing too many new concepts to grasp all at once, I was anxious to leave the church and feel fresh air. I wanted to step out of the stale thoughts and energies floating around in this church and sit in nature again, next to alive, growing trees and to smell flowers. I wanted to come back into the present moment of my life.

I passed the restaurant set in the beautiful garden between the Villa Bethany and below the Tour Magdala where people sat eating their lunch under the tall pines. The smell of grilled chicken reached my nose as I passed, but I wanted only to stand below the Tour Magdala.

Crouching down against its stone foundation, I closed my eyes. A soft breath of freshness, a moment of inner peace welled within my heart. Minutes passed before I opened my eyes to marvel at the landscape and the mountains in the distance, capped with snow-covered peaks, the Pyrenees.

Shortly after Ann came over to tell me Alena wanted to take us into the graveyard behind the church so I got up and followed her back. As we passed the Magdalene Church, Alexis pointed out what was written above the entrance, in Latin. "Terrible is this Place." But it wasn't until we were standing in front of the unusually designed arched doorway to the graveyard that we discussed it.

"Shocking words" I said almost at the same time as two other women while turning up my mouth. "No", said Alena smiling, "It really means, 'This is a wonderful, awesome place'." "Is it some kind of slang way of saying something?" I asked. But then I remembered when I was teaching photography in Harlem, New York, and when a student admired a shirt or pair of pants another student was wearing, he or she would say emphatically, "That's bad!"

However I had to wonder why anything so bizarre would be written before the entrance of a church. I began asking myself, *How many hidden mysteries are there here anyway? Do I really want to know them all?*

Clearly something unknown to most people was hidden here and it was probably why early researchers began blowing up places around the village looking for the entrances to these lost treasures, until dynamite was outlawed at Rennes Le Chateau in 1956.

As we walked inside the graveyard, the largest and most obvious grave was opposite the door so we walked over to it. Alena said it was the grave of Madame Hautpoul who had been the last royal family member who lived here; she died on January 17, 1781. Curiously, the writings on her gravestone were defaced by Abbe Sauniere a hundred years later. There was a bigger story here. Alena decided to give us a little bit of it.

She told us that the Magdalene church was originally a private chapel belonging to the lords of Rennes Le Chateau as part of their castle. It was almost in ruins by the time Berenger Saunier arrived at the turn of the century, so he began renovating the church. Alexis told us that the priest who preceded Sauniere, Abbe Bigou, had a long relationship with the noble family. Evidently it extended back to his priest father before him.

But just before the French Revolution when he departure for Spain, Abbe Bigou carved coded writings on Madame Hautpoul's headstone. It was ten years after she had died.

Alena told us that Abbe Sauniere then defaced the coded writings on this headstone, which at the time, people guessed was because he received the secret message Abbe Bigou had left for him. What that was however, is still a mystery.

Whew, I thought to myself, *I have heard much too much on my first experience up here,* as we departed.

Yet my thoughts still lingered on what this coded message might have said.

As our van descended down the steep hill, Alena quickly remembered something and turned to us declaring, "Oh, I forgot to mention, Rennes Le Chateau is also known to have been the location of an ancient Temple of Isis." That got my attention.

Chapter 14 – La Pique

The next day we would have a very different experience. We would be going to the center of the pentagram in the landscape, that long limestone ridge leading to La Pique Alena had pointed out from the Tour Magdala. Again we drove off onto a remote winding dirt road to where the long ridge began. Jay parked the van in a grassy cove over which several young oak trees spread their branches. As we each gathered our backpacks to meet under the trees, Alena spread a blanket for the picnic our chef had prepared. We were all invited to create our own French style sandwich.

Hungry, I reached for part of a baguette, cut a hearty slice of soft brie cheese, added a slice of pate, several slices of tomato and then grabbed a handful of soft lettuce. Arranging it carefully, I closed it, took a bite and strolled off to look around.

Alena had given us a nice overview from the Tour Magdala so we were aware of the names of the two mountains, Mt Bugarach and Pech Cardou. She had also pointed out Bezu, where a Knights Templar 'commanderie' had been. They surrounded us in the distance, each located on one of the pentagram points.

Interestingly, as I strolled around eating my sandwich, I glanced up at a small hill when I heard a faint voice inside my head instruct me to walk up this hill. So I did and looked out from its high point in other directions, not knowing if I was supposed to see something unusual. I admired the beauty from there but after walking back down I went over to the group who were laughing loudly amongst themselves.

Quickly, a Priestess from Tucson ran over to me and pointed to the top of the hill where I'd been, asking, "Who were those beings you were talking to up on that hill," she stammered, "the ones wearing those white robes?"

Without hesitation I replied, "What beings in white robes? I have no idea who you're talking about." Having no recollection of anything happening up there, I did recall the little voice inside that instructed me to walk up the hill. Now that I had a witness who could see things in other realms, it was curious that I hadn't even seen them myself.

After finishing our lunch we each crossed the dirt road to step onto the rocks marking the beginning of the limestone ridge. It would lead us to the center of this famous five-pointed star in the landscape.

Down the straight path we walked closer and closer to the end. Who could ever imagine that we would be stepping into the center of a forty mile wide star-shaped pattern laid out in the landscape? Evidently no one knew who built it or why. Slightly nervous I realized that maybe I was about to step into some lost dimension or reality here.

I knew Venus was the only planet that made the geometric symbol of a five-pointed star in the heavens, but it took exactly eight years to perform. Thus I wondered if she might have a connection or a claim to this landscape temple.

It became an exhilarating experience as we walked single file to the end point. Some did so quietly, others not, pointing and sharing their first impressions with others who listened. Then we arrived at the end.

There were no trees; we were totally exposed to the mystical mountains and the surrounding points in every direction. Below to the left was a tall vertical rock, appearing as if it were a guardian figure. It had a long distinct face and recessed areas for the eyes. The seeming helmet-like attachment surrounding its head gave the impression that it was a figure mysteriously guarding something important.

Then we took turns standing at the end point. Each of us either twisted to face in each direction, or just stood still looking in one direction. When it was my turn I turned to face Rennes Le Chateau. Shocked I watched four pillars of white light streaking up and out from within the hill, as if they were reaching up to the heavens high above. Excited, I knew these were the same four pillars of light I'd seen while we first drove up to Rennes Le Chateau.

But suddenly these four pillars of light, all at the same time, arched over from the top and turned into rainbows of light as if they were hands reaching out to invite something to enter inside. It was as if they were forming a chalice waiting to be filled up. *Was this an invitation for Venus to enter this landscape pentagram and claim her sacred temple*, I questioned?

As I looked back to the beginning of my France journey, I had experienced many intriguing moments like this and heard many new stories while hoping to be touched by Mary Magdalene's presence. In fact I noticed other Priestess sisters in quiet moments of thought also trying to integrate a new insight or fact they learned, hoping to discern what was true and what had value for them. I knew I was ready to open my heart wider to embrace a bigger picture of the path before me.

There was an ancient memory calling me here, enticing me to return, not only from the past life regression Alena did but from the visions I'd had in Rennes Les Bains before the group arrived.

We danced a lot on our journey, expressing ourselves to the gentle rhythmic Hawaiian music as if it were our theme song. Not only had we graced vineyards and our hotel dining room with dance, most significantly our dancing graced the field below the Tour Magdala. This is where the magic happened that bound each of us together, through the mounting passion of our ecstatic dance.

It was here we felt the whales and dolphins being summoned by the power of our Priestess dance. The vibrations descended into the depths of the great mother. The last day I wrote this poem hoping to embrace with words my story, our story:

> I've seen into the light and I've seen into the dark
> But my greatest vision was of the Arc
> We were a coven – a net of women
> Dancing out loud intensely driven
> We were doing our work in an ancient time
> In a special circle
> Around something hidden and sublime
> Our lives were simple
> Set deep within the rocks
> As we dressed in robes of white and pale yellow frocks
> The knowledge we carried was from a far away star
> That others might think just too far out or bizarre
> Now we've come back with promise and laughter
> And incredible zeal
> To find that place of the heart
> And to help the feminine heal
> It was the sound of the trumpet
> The sign of the Dove
> That has summoned us from our source above
> Magdalene has called us to bring our wings
> So we can learn again all those ancient things

We've danced on the Earth and reached to the stars
Listening to Aloha music blasting from our falcon
car
The whales and Dolphins have heard our plea
And have begun to unite under the sea
We are weaving bridges of light and harmony
So thanks to you and thanks to me
And to all of us who can see
That she needs us now to pilot the ships
And to help arc the rainbow of the covenant
It is you Magdalene who has brought us here
Because you sense the quickening
So we have set our vows and tried to be clear
Our work has begun and we have no fear
And we'll look forward to the coming years
Will it unfold here?

Chapter 15 - Emerging As My Priestess Self

My left shoulder bare, I was wearing an indigo dress with small silver half moons dangling from my belt. A circular doubled string of pearls, was on my head like a crown and a small amethyst crystal extended from it over my third eye above my eyebrows.

It was everything my feminine guide suggested I wear weeks earlier when I walked up to communicate with her. She resided high up within the tall rock spire I called Isis in the front of Sedona's Thunder Mountain.

I was going to be ordained, to emerge as a Priestess with eight other women. Finishing our final ceremony of *rebirthing,* I was supported to move beyond old limitations, any unresolved issues and those that didn't belong to me. I was ready to step out into the world as my new Priestess self.

During our last meeting in Flagstaff we finalized details and questions concerning the ceremony. Each woman could chose to either align and be ordained through the Fellowship of Isis from Ireland carrying the older traditions or to be ordained through the Celestial Earth, Nicole's "Iseum" and become a new Priestess to the World. Or we could do both.

While reflecting on both possibilities, I drove down through the canyon, following the road as it turned like a snake trying to uncoil itself, before it emptied into uptown Sedona. I was filled with a new joy, a peace after all I had unraveled during the process.

"Oh No," I said when suddenly, as I came around a hairpin turn at the bottom of the canyon, a car came from the opposite lane, heading directly at me. As I clutched the wheel, my heart raced with terror. Another energy took over almost as if it was an unknown force within me. It grasped the steering wheel and swerved my car off the road while the other car quickly moved back inside the sharp turn and passed me by.

Panicked I stayed there until my heartbeat settled back into a normal rhythm. Paused in this terrifying moment, my life at stake, I quickly looked in to see if this incident had a deeper meaning.

Yes, I saw a male figure appear from an ancient time, a past life, and I knew or felt as if he was attempting to stop me from claiming my Priestess identity in this life. He had been amongst the masculine forces that came in to destroy the Priestess temples in Egypt, sometimes even killing the women as they ran. It was that lifetime when the patriarchy came in to take control. But now after more than 2000 years I was ready to reclaim my lost heritage.

Family, friends and others were gathered to witness our Ordination. Some were seated, others standing, in the backyard area that had been prepared for our ceremony at one of the Priestess' homes. We were cool under the tall ponderosa pine trees of Flagstaff this hot July afternoon.

As the ceremony began, one by one, each woman was invited to come stand in front of the facilitator, Aleia, who would ask her:

What gift are you offering to the Goddess?

She would deliver her gift to the Goddess, a poem she had written or sing a song she liked and one or two performed a dance she had choreographed. Afterword she was asked to state her intention, what she was bringing to the world as a Priestess. When it was my turn, two Priestess sisters sang my favorite song while I offered my dance.

My head bowed, my eyes covered, they began. Slowly I lifted my head and deliberately glided around in a circle honoring each direction, before stooping down to touch and honor the Earth Mother. Then I reached my bare arms high above to the places of origin in the cosmos.

As I gracefully moved into the center of the circle, my head was raised, my eyes wide as my arms were open to the universe, the song ended. I held the gesture for seconds in stillness before walking over to stand before Aleia.

She acknowledged my dance on behalf of the Goddess then asked if I had something to proclaim, what I would be stepping into as a Priestess. Reaching for my carefully written paper nearby I began, but first declaring that I received my priestess name during that first journey in France.

I AM Priestess Of Remembrance And Vision Of The One
Be it known on this planet Earth,
In all dimensions and realms,
And on other planets
That uphold the Divine lineage
Of the Feminine principle,
That I, Nancy Safford, carry this lineage forth
Imparting it to others for the highest good of all,
Through the purest devotion, intent and love,
That we may co-exist on planet Earth
In harmony, compassion and complete fulfillment,
Balanced in the male/female principles
That originate from the ONE source.
I Vow To Uphold And Carry The Divine Light Of
Remembrance

To Help Illuminate All Beings Into Oneness

Aleia walked over in front of me and began her words of ordination, accepting my proclamation. To seal it she anointed my forehead, my heart and the top of my head with the anointing oil Spikenard, to represent the ancient priestess traditions in Egypt. Then she wrapped the wings of Isis around me by extending her arms from behind. "They will always protect you on your path."

Although this Ceremony of Emergence-Ordination had been completed it was actually just the beginning. In fact our proclamations would take a year and a day to be fully anchored as we each stepped into our *Priestess* vibration.

*Whew...*I said to myself when the ceremony was over. Feeling lighter, a new sense of joy in my heart, I was ready to celebrate with my newly ordained Priestess sisters.

Our friends, families, husbands and children had all witnessed the ceremony. We drank toasts of sparkling cider and wine then feasted on the many luscious salads, freshly grown tomatoes, meats, cheeses and ripe summer fruits.. I smiled a lot because it had been a long, intense nine months. After releasing myself from old patterns and beliefs, I was ready to birth myself into something new, more authentic.

Truthfully my journey into the feminine mysteries began the day that elusive figure appeared above the creek waters of Sedona and invited me to follow her. She was my first vision and it has not stopped.

Embracing the Priestess energy was leading me now. I knew it was my calling, my passion. It was my life's purpose. That little voice inside who had led me here could finally relax.

By continuously doing my inner work and shamanic practices, I gained more discernment in working with these other realities. I became more responsible for myself, acknowledging that Robert had done a lot on my behalf, probably more than I would ever know.

Months later I formed my own Iseum in Sedona through the Fellowship of Isis in Ireland. I called it the Isis Iseum of the Heart. That way I had my own organization through which I could also offer a similar process for other women. Continuing Nicole's lineage meant I would facilitate a similar process but adding my own vision to it; the core principal remained the same.

Lastly, at the end of the first process another level had begun, Awakening the Magdalene Within, also designed by Nicole. She would be introducing it in Flagstaff in the fall just months after my ordination. I, eager to continue to the next level, enrolled. It would be exploring the wisdom and hidden truths of Mary Magdalene.

At the same time Nicole invited me to co-facilitate the first group to be introduced in Sedona, *Awakening the Priestess Within.* She would come up from Tucson once a month for a long Saturday with the new initiates and I would facilitate the one evening or afternoon session a month usually doing some kind of ceremony. I offered Robert's and my house under Thunder Mountain for both sessions.

Chapter 16 – Lady Olivia Returns

Appearing in a silvery-blue shimmering light, a figure made a visit to me while I was in meditation. To see this figure brought tears to my eyes. Then I heard her say, *I am Ishtar… and my wisdom has always been true. I will be with you very soon.* Then she was gone. As her essence lingered in my heart it felt like something had happened to me, and it seemed like my heart wanted to break open. Anxiously I waited, wondering when that would be.

Two weeks later Lady Olivia arrived to participate in Sedona's first Priestess group, the one Nicole had invited me to co-facilitate. I was excited, hoping to engage her in a new experience, doing something she hadn't done before. In fact, I invited Lady Olivia to join the group, when I was facilitating, to participate in a medicine wheel ceremony. Not knowing how to do the actual ceremony myself, I invited one of the Priestess initiates who did, to facilitate it.

Rachel's Knoll was a special place high up in Long Canyon, one of Sedona's many canyons that the owner had designated for meditation and some ceremonies. And it had a large medicine wheel.

The medicine wheel was a circle formed with various sized rocks laid on the earth. Traditionally one enters it from the east, and then the other directions were marked with large rocks, the south, the west and then the north. Then a pathway led to the small center circle where the last two directions were usually honored, the above and the below.

Several people in Sedona offered medicine wheel ceremonies, so I had experienced it several times and learned a little background. It was a Native American ceremony practiced mostly by the plains tribes who used it as a cyclic teaching. They designated the four directions, the four seasons, the four times of day and then related it to the human life cycle.

I knew it would be a new experience for Lady Olivia because she had not explored these native traditions. They were so different from anything in Ireland, her home country. In the last part of our ceremony Lady Olivia, after watching everyone have their turn in the center of the wheel, walked inside it to have her own.

Standing where Mother Earth and Father Sky came together, she began to honor the directions. Her right arm reached out to gather the east and southern directions and then her left hand reached back to gather the west and northern directions, as she then brought them all into her heart. She said a quiet prayer and then closed her eyes.

Her short figure was dressed in a long patterned blue skirt, enhanced with a red shawl over her shoulders, though one side had slipped lower than the other after her sweeping arm motions. Standing quietly in the center with her eyes closed, surely she was lost in other worlds. Finally, she opened her eyes.

One eye was looking off to the side, unfocused, as it has been since she was very young, while her other eye, brown, calmly looked ahead. Then she walked out from the center, circled it a few times to seal her prayers and then went back to stand in her place in the north.

After everyone had stood in the middle and said their prayer, it was over. The animal guides were thanked, released and everyone walked out of the wheel.

"Wonderful, just wonderful," Lady Olivia exclaimed to us, in her strong English accent, convincing us all how much she had loved the experience.

When everyone had departed, she and I remained. We walked over to the other side of Rachel's Knoll facing the high white limestone and sandstone rock formation most of us called the Temple of Isis. I wanted Lady Olivia to experience it.

A tall juniper tree with a twisted trunk stood behind a wooden bench where some visitors liked to sit gazing out at the expansive landscape. However, Lady Olivia almost in a trance, chose to stand beside the tree while I perched myself on the edge of this bench. Quiet, we each slipped into our own stillness lost in the timeless mystery of the canyon before us.

Suddenly something started moving in front of me. As I engaged my other senses, it seemed like there were wings flapping, when minutes later I sensed a being gliding down in front of me. I heard the words,
I am with you now! Discerning carefully with my other vision, I saw a tall bird-like figure standing there flapping its wings softly.

As fast as the words would come out I called to Lady Olivia. "Please come over, come over here. I think this is Isis landing." She scurried over next to me and I told her the words I heard. Silently, she stood still for a few minutes. "Yes, yes she is here," agreeing with what I saw and felt.

Then I told her about the figure who had called herself Ishtar appearing before me two weeks earlier and the words she spoke to me.
"Yes," Lady Olivia said, "Ishtar is another form of Isis. And yes others called her by different names. But Ishtar also represents Isis."

I was deeply honored to have Lady Olivia standing next to me as Isis- Ishtar acknowledged that she was *with me now*, validating that she indeed came down as a white winged bird figure.

Moreover Lady Olivia believed that Isis was initially the Goddess of 10,000 names and that each carried an attribute of the One Goddess. She encouraged all of us to align with other names and qualities of Isis that might also call to us, such as Bridget, Rhiannon or Mary Magdalene.

During this visit Lady Olivia also did a special ceremony for Nicole. She wanted to elevate her to another status, a "Hierophant," identified as a person who stood in a position to oversee others in the Fellowship of Isis. The ceremony was to honor Nicole for the ongoing work she had done and was continuing to do in the world. It was also because she had expanded the first level of the priestess process by creating *Awakening the Magdalene Within.* Afterword, Lady Olivia left for California to participate in ceremonies performed with other groups working with Isis and who were connected to the Fellowship.

Chapter 17 – Awakening the Magdalene Within

As I began the next level of the priestess process, *Awakening The Magdalene Within*, Nicole informed our small group that by reclaiming archetypes Mary Magdalene symbolized, we would be reclaiming another part of our lost feminine spirit. It was the part connecting our sexual and spiritual natures.

Consciously, the Catholic Church had been calling Mary Magdalene a prostitute for nearly 2000 years now, suppressing the sexuality of the feminine nature. Seemingly, it was to divert the outer world from recognizing who she truly was, what she stood for.

By activating the Magdalene life force energy, Nicole hoped it would help us resolve feelings of separation and self-judgments from long ago. When we began addressing the difference between the *sacred* and the *profane* aspects of our sexual nature, I sensed how this nine month process would have me dig up memories I'd squashed in some lost corner of my heart hoping to forget.

She facilitated ways to bring memories deep in our psyches into the light, sometimes referring to the book, *The Sacred Prostitute, Eternal Aspect of The Feminine,* by Nancy Qualls-Corbett, as we began working with archetypes.

As I looked more deeply at my sexuality and values, almost immediately it brought up feelings of shame. I saw that some shame came from the passion I felt during intimate moments of making love, as if exploring my feeling this way was not acceptable. If ever I stepped into a church, it got worse, when the thought of having sex felt unclean, as if it were taboo.

The Catholic Church and other Christian churches had spiritualized the positive attributes of the Goddess when they made her the Holy Virgin or the Holy Mother. She became untouchable as they elevated her to the highest heavenly heights. Love became so ethereal that no aspect of sensuality could be associated with it.

Furthermore recognition of the body and any earthly desires associated with it, like physical love and passion, disappeared. It was as if our sexual nature had to be hidden as women were then viewed as "destructive" their sexuality "devilish."

Our continuing sessions helped me to gain a better understanding of my more authentic self. We did ceremonies and a lot of writing. In fact, during one exercise, we were asked to write messages from our vaginas, using the opposite hand to write. That way the message could be heard without our mind interfering.

After doing this, I could barely read my crazy illegible script. I recognized however, that it had a few things to say:

Are you here? Please help me to evolve. I want you to get to the right place so you truly know who I am. I can bring you such beauty and fulfillment. Please make me an altar and ask that I be able to show you love, ecstasy, now. It will release your hold on my expression.

Whooo, I said to myself after, it definitely seemed to be telling me that I had cut it off from its true expression. I mused on how my body parts could speak such truths.

In another session I especially liked hearing the stories about early temple life when women's lives were focused on being in alignment with a higher consciousness. Evidently Priestess lineages flowed through the early temples, from 2000 years ago as the traditional wisdom was passed down.

We explored the value of several archetypes like the *Love Goddess* who Nicole explained was once revered as the one who renewed and brought passion and fertility to all life, including sexual encounters between men and women.

Focusing on the sacred prostitute who lived in these temple communities, she was in close connection to the great goddess by keeping sacred her ceremonies and places on the land, the waters.

In her book, *The Sacred Prostitute*, Nancy Qualls-Corbett writes:

"Women who chose not to marry spent their lives in the temple compounds. Referred to as the 'Vestal Virgins' these women did not unite with a husband, their feminine nature was dedicated to a higher purpose. She, as Priestess often became the 'bride' in a ritual marriage, referred to as a 'hieros gamos' ceremony, when she was chosen to embody the Goddess, as her fertile womb. The God, embodied by the reigning monarch in this ritual, would be assured fertility and well-being for his lands, his domain, and his people."

"These Vestal Virgins served the Goddess of Greece and Rome, as Hestia and Vesta, as they tended the hearth fires. The hearth, known as 'the omphalos,' was the feminine hub of the universe and considered the navel stone of the temple." [3]

The book also spoke about the profane prostitute who represented the dark side of sexuality. For millennia her life was centered in brothels, taverns and places of sexual entertainment. She was not allowed in the temples or to participate in religious ceremony.

In her degradation she was the antithesis of the sacred prostitute whose sexuality revered the Goddess. Yet they existed in juxtaposition. It was curious what led some to the temple of love and others to the brothel.

While exploring details of this early temple life, Nicole had someone lead us through a past life regression so we could go back and possibly experience a lifetime from this period in history.

Sure enough, I connected with a time when I'd been immersed in the Goddess traditions as a young Priestess, living in a temple and given specific teachings that detached me from physical feelings of love and passion.

But then I fell in love with a man who frequented the temple. Soon after, in accordance with my family's traditions, and after finishing my temple duties I left the temple and was married off to another man.

Then I was caught going against my "duties and obligations" as a wife, by indulging myself in my newfound passion for the man I met in the temple. Socially demeaned, I was then symbolically shamed for it.

At that time marriages were contracts without concern if there was love. But it felt like I had been sent into the 'underworld' to be with the dark goddess where I, and my psyche have been lost for centuries, probably millennia. No one came to get me.

Thanks to our Magdalene process, I was able to identify her hidden in my subconscious and able to perform a shamanic soul retrieval to reclaim her. I offered the dark goddess a large pink crystal in exchange.

Sadly, it appeared that my self-judgment and guilt for loving someone, having sexual passion, had been lingering in my subconscious for thousands of years. Now I was beginning to have a glimmer of how my physical feelings could be connected to my spiritual self, that part of me re-emerging from all my priestess awakenings. My earlier experiences of female figures appearing to me, helped me connect to my spiritual self.

In our next session we worked with the concept of sacred union the uniting of opposites, like the masculine and feminine, spirit and matter, our sexuality and spirituality. Nicole hoped we could establish harmony within ourselves.

First she asked us to draw the image of our inner male, so I asked that he show me his face. When he did I discovered something dark lurking behind him. It scared me. Questioning how long it had been hiding there, I received no answer. Then it occurred to me, *Maybe it had arrived in another lifetime like the one I'd just seen?*

Drawing my inner female self, I saw how small she was. Possibly she'd been hiding from what was behind the inner male. Obviously I had work to do to re-establish an inner relationship between them. By waking up my sexuality and desires, the Magdalene process invited me to look at how I had been in the world with previous partners and lovers.

I identified how there had always been a relationship in my life, since my late teens. Sometimes it was with an older man, sometimes a younger one and then yes, with a few married men. I had been like a racehorse, running forward, never sideways or backwards. When I was over with one relationship, I stepped into another, without much reflection about who had been affected, hurt.

Now, I was ready to account for my reckless ways, recognizing that I had been hiding from real love. Perhaps I hadn't been ready for the real thing, whatever that was.

Looking at what was surfacing from my first archetypes, my mother, stepmother and father and their beliefs about love I thought perhaps I was carrying something from them that was not mine as I looked deeper into who I was at my core.

My guidance to Mary Magdalene, I thought was to better understand lost archetypes she represented, the priestess, the sacred prostitute, the spiritual woman. By unveiling the secrets surrounding her life, like her wisdom and spirituality, and her real relationship with Jesus, I thought it might help me in mine.

Totally absorbed in my *Awakening The Magdalene Within* process, I attempted to hold onto an outer image of myself. Trying to appear as if I were calm, stable and grounded, my issues were tearing me up inside.

It was as if my heart was suddenly cracking open and my protective shields were falling away, like I had become an earthquake ready to erupt. Hidden deep in my heart, frozen like an iceberg, my true feelings were surfacing. They were melting and I was being given a glimpse inside. Alone, I wanted to be alone.

Suddenly, there it was. Yes...it was about being vulnerable. I was afraid of my vulnerability. It was my fear of being hurt, to feel pain in my heart. I thought it would destroy me if I loved someone too deeply so I kept my distance.

In complete turmoil, I chose to move over to my little cottage in Oak Creek to be alone so I could better address these issues. Months earlier, I had rented it to do my shamanic sessions with clients. It was beautifully situated above the waters of Sedona's Oak Creek Canyon.

Robert was supportive on so many levels, but he was having a few health issues himself, so I moved over to deal with my issues without involving him, or anyone else. I know he was confused, not understanding as fully as I would have hoped, but it was what I had to do.

I brought over my futon bed and a small desk to continue my life there as conveniently as possible, not sure how long I would be here.

On my journey to know the core of my feminine self, all I could do was   surrender. I knew nothing. No one could tell me what the true feminine was supposed to be, or even look like, but most importantly, no one could tell me what it was supposed to *feel like*. Furthermore, I dedicated the next part of my life to this search.

My intention had been that Robert and I would get back together, however, as I continued on my ever-forward search, it never happened. We remained friends, although he was very hurt and also probably angry at me.

Several months after our *Awakening the Magdalene Within* process was over, Nicole claimed it unwise for anyone to make big decisions or changes in their relationships during the process. Since ours was only the second or third one she had offered, she was still working out the protocol.

No matter what she might have recommended, I had to do what I did. There was too much for me to see and hopefully clear in order to re-focus my life. I always kept in touch with Robert, as he was very important to me. I was saddened in my heart and prayed that he could understand why I had to do what I did.

Near the end of our nine months of sessions, when it had warmed up, instead of doing all our sessions in Flagstaff at one of the participants' house, we met and performed a few spontaneous ceremonies at my cottage in Oak Creek.

For one of them Nicole used the symbolic shape of the spiral. One person would be selected to stand at the beginning of the spiral to symbolically go deep into the hidden mysteries and bring them out. Then the others would form the curves of the spiral to assist in bringing them out.

Curiously, I was the one selected to stand at the beginning of this spiral as we all stood in the shallow water activating it. We would be bridging the ceremony with the temple in France, because I had begun to receive visions and seemingly lost information and had mentioned it to Nicole.

This ceremony was in perfect timing, as I was about to leave for my next visit to France. It would be after co-facilitating a Glastonbury trip with two new friends. Thus, I was curious to learn what information I might encounter there to bring back.

Chapter 18 - Rennes Le Chateau, A Second Time

In the same room, the same hotel, in the same village, Rennes Les Bains, it was as if I never left. This second trip would be a short one, a week, as I'd just finished co-facilitating a ten day journey to Glastonbury for a New Zealand group. While I was guiding them around Sedona they had expressed interest in the ancient Goddess sites of Glastonbury. Thus already being in England, I would fly to France after in late August of 1997.

It was after lunch when I stepped out the heavy French doors into the August heat. Remembering my way to the bridge arched over the Sals River, I paused next to the potted pink and purple petunias as their sweet scent touched my senses.

Looking down at the river I spotted two women with children in the hot bath area. The stone bathtub squeezed them together, the two women, their children in the middle, as the hot waters flowed out from the hole in the ancient rock wall.

On the other side of the bridge I turned left and found the dirt path over the tiny footbridge to the Little Cascade, hoping more intriguing images would be shown to me, like before.

I climbed to a semicircular area, where rocks were braced against the dirt banks as water cascaded from above into the little pond. Nearby was a fig tree bursting with ripe fruit. I moved over to secure a comfortable spot, my back against the intimate enclave, where I settled into this long awaited moment. Warm pockets of air touched my shoulders and heart, enhancing my welcome.

Within a short time, I found myself responding to a soft stimulation, a sensation that seemed to wake up the lower area of my body, my lower chakras, my sexual energies.

Having reclaimed so many of my Priestess memories, quickly I wondered if this had been a Temple area. Maybe I was sitting near one of the entrances and fantasized if, in ancient times, it was a ceremonial place where Priestesses once honored their feminine cycles. Undoubtedly it had been a place to celebrate a Priestess's first blood, her first sexuality, I realized, as I continued to have more sensations in my lower chakras.

Then I got up and chose to stroll along the river, before going back to my room for the night. It was early evening and still light as I laid down on my small bed, when I fell into, what felt like, some kind of eternal sleep, from which my eyes only opened the next morning.

Finally awake, I sat up, hoping to grasp the image 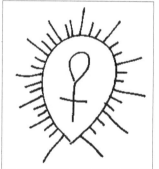 from a lucid dream I'd just had. Suspended and glistening in front of me was an Egyptian Ankh symbol, floating inside a tear shaped form as rays of light streamed out around it. Nearby, was a tall, timeless figure, a female, seemingly from long ago. I grabbed my journal and quickly drew it.

Knowing that the Ankh symbol represented "life" in Egypt and that reliefs depicted Gods and Isis holding the Ankh, I learned that it symbolized life and death, thus, that they were immortal. If the Ankh symbolized the waters, the springs, from which they believed came the elixir of immortality, then to hold the Ankh was to drink from the well.

But wanting to have a more in depth explanation, I found some writings from a researcher, Laird Scranton who claims:

The Ankh can no longer be viewed as just meaning 'life'. It is the creation of life itself. The Secret of the Ankh is a pathway into the Mystery Systems...in line with the Infinity Puzzle...as Egyptians knew of one creator...the one who arose out of the primordial ocean. Thus the secret of the Ankh is here. It is about structures, the structure of matter, and about the structure of reproduction and genetics. [4]

As I reflected on this information, it was curious that we had just done a spiral ceremony in our Magdalene group, before I left for England, then France. The beginning of our spiral was sourced directly in the creek waters, where I stood. Thus, it was intended for me to bring forth more information from deep within the temple. Nicole knew I had already begun doing this in France.

After finishing breakfast, a crispy croissant that melted in my mouth, and swallowing a few freshly picked figs, black ones, I, in the busy hotel dining room, pushed my corner table seat back, stood up and hiked up to my room to change into my sandals.

Once down the hotel stairs and out the front door, I walked across the arched bridge over the Sals River where a group of teenagers were laughing together in the hot bathtub below. I was ready for my next adventure at the magical Little Cascade.

Passing a small apple tree situated on the bank around the pond, I sat down cross-legged on a square rock facing it, as the waters emptied into it from above.

I reached my hand into the water lifting some onto my face, bathing it with coolness, before I put a few drops on my heart and settled back into the stillness. Again, that smooth, calm stimulation began to affect my lower chakras; I questioned what was so actively stored in the land here.

Oh! I said. Something was moving above the water before me. My vision took over as I quickly noticed one spiral-like strand begin to unbraid itself before me into two strands, two columns moving around, as if they were dancing with each other. They resembled two snakes that were intertwined. Then I received a message:

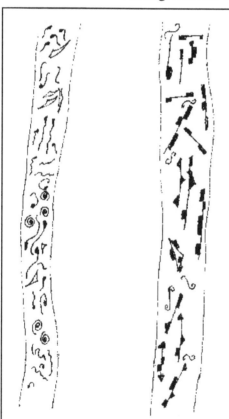

From one comes two then from two comes one. The DNA strands you have drawn are codes from elsewhere. Together they

create the Egg from which comes life. Life is an 'Egg of Blessing', until we experience separation and cannot remember the One.

I grabbed my pen and paper (always with me now) to draw them. Complicated forms and symbols were inside each one, very different from each other I noticed, as my hands moved fast to draw each within its own vertical line.

Realizing that indeed, I might easily have connected with an aspect of the early temple life here, the following morning, I awoke to discover my blood had started flowing. My "period" was two weeks early, but I knew traveling and changing time zones often alters body rhythms. I thought it would last only as long as I was in France, four or five more days.

Later that day, curious about this experience, I asked my inner guides to look more deeply into it, when a goddess figure dressed in white appeared wearing a crown, a crystal at each point. She was standing next to a tree by the water and called me *daughter,* explaining:

These places were ancient ones of sexuality, in a more complicated way than one might believe. What you are experiencing here at Rennes Les Bains, could be dangerous, without a good knowledge of kundalini energy, as the sexual energy could get stuck. When it is channeled as a group of women with joined hearts, it's one thing, but by an individual it's another.

The feminine "vagina" is much more than we would ever have known. The act of sex from love, if done in the Priestess vibration, can connect the act with galaxies far beyond ours. Crowns, when worn with specific crystals on their points, can be applied for each galaxy. A Priestess can connect wherever she is guided to go in the heavens, and can take her partner on a journey of initiation.

For instance, if one is looking for the initiation of the moon, it is about the ebb and flow of light, the ups and downs of our emotions, feelings and passions. Thus there is an endless surrender, like going into the ocean, with its undulating waves.

This message was unlike anything I could have imagined. Reflecting on it, I gave thanks, realizing that it was time to learn more about kundalini and tantric practices.

However, what happened was the bleeding continued long after my return to Sedona and wouldn't stop. Panicked after three weeks, I got scared and had to find help; a woman specializing in herbs and remedies gave me something that stopped it. Interestingly, the energy had gotten stuck in my second chakra area, as this figure speaking to me mentioned happening.

With only a few days left in this magical village before returning to Sedona, I wanted to explore the five thousand year old Seat of Isis, situated on a path high above Rennes Les Bains. People have named it such, but actually it is called the *Fauteil du Diable*, or The Devil's Armchair. Nothing was written about any association with Asmodeus, but he was the only figure referred to as the "Devil" in the area, crouched inside the entrance at the Rennes Le Chateau church.

After getting specific instructions from the woman at the hotel, I had three choices of paths to reach this Seat Of Isis. I chose a route that crossed the same bridge over the Salz River, where at the point of choice, I turned right.

Following this paved path, I passed the old hotel over the hot baths, and then stone houses against the embankment on my left, before there were no more buildings. Bending and then straightening several times, the path continued, as the fresh summer air enlivened me.

At a low bridge, I crossed to find a two-way road, then an upward driveway to a stone house, where it would cease. Turning abruptly at this last house, next to an orchard of twisted apple trees, I found the obscured path. A narrow dirt trail, it went up, leaving all vestiges of people, cars and houses behind.

Climbing over partially buried rocks in the earth in pursuit of Isis' sacred chair, I found mulberries hanging on trees here and there, as wild rose bushes perfumed the air. In fact I bent down to pick a dark pink one as an offering to Isis.

Then at a small clearing, I saw a large rounded stone, isolated, ahead on the path. Passing between two narrow birch trees, I asked permission to enter this seemingly sacred temple area. Approaching reverently, I spotted a tiny heart–shaped basin of water, into which the spring behind poured its waters. Luscious green ferns grew around this spring I noticed, bending down to place the rose in the water basin, asking Isis to be with me here.

Alena had informed our group that for five thousand years this seat had presumably waited for people to sit and discover its mysteries. She said it offered initiations to those who were ready. Isolated, it was set off by itself, as the path twisted around it and continued up above a dangerous drop-off that had been scooped out from centuries of harsh weather.

Silently, I moved over to this carved chair, her seat, and bowed. Then I climbed into it. My feet didn't touch the ground, as it was big, just like a throne with wide rests for my arms and plenty of room for any sized candidate. I sat closing my eyes gently. The only sound was the tree branches rustling back and forth above me.

Within minutes it began. Spirals...one from above, one from below appeared. I was in the middle of something. The armchair kept me grounded. Many sensations enveloped my body, stirred my inner energies before I felt my heart became lighter and that my solar plexus had freed itself of hidden anxieties. The top of my head, my eyes and neck felt cleared. It was as if I was on a ride, lifted up, into something unique, while just sitting in this ancient chair.

I settled back in my body, relaxing but there seemed to be something above me, lingering. Carefully I slipped into my inner vision. Whereby I saw a giant eye floating there, with what seemed to be eyelashes, suspended. I stretched my hands up, wide, opening to whomever and whatever it was, giving thanks for my powerful experience, after which I was ready to climb down. But no, it seemed someone wanted to speak to me, so I settled back down and listened:

It was twenty-two thousand years ago when I was granted permission to bring life here on this planet. I was innocent in my approach and desired the best experience for all. It seemed easy to recreate what I AM and have known as life, consciousness, though we had no names for our states of being then. I knew what it was and thought it could be created, re-created easily.

From my seat, I was the guardian of worlds that surrounded me as pearls on a necklace of light. I took the responsibility to create a world with beings capable of activating the same energy that I could hold.

When, like a bolt of lightning, I seeded this place it was from my place above the waters. The lightning brought the waters up from the Earth as my light traveled down and marked places sacred in these waters.

I made an archway of light in each place where the lightning struck, as water sources were created - springs and wells. They were the places I marked by light. That's what we are you know, water and light. Sometimes one will proceed the other, but we are simultaneous with our creation of life here on Earth.

Then, like buttons on a vest, called by light, the sisters arrived. There are seven parts, seven bridges to the center in Rennes Les Bains... our Pod... the 'Place of Origin' here. This is a Natural Doorway, a way to love, eternity, bliss. Here is where I sit. Here is where we began.

We are the Guardians of Life here. We are the keepers of the 'Stone'. Only we can touch it. Do you know who I AM? I Am all that is was or ever has been. I Am all around you, but do you know it? Not yet, you search though. I call you all to surrender to me. I Am in the last place that you will look, within yourself.

Not totally present in my body after, I gently stepped down from her timeless *chair,* turned, bowed and gave thanks. I descended the narrow path to find my way into town. Choosing a different return route, I went directly into Rennes Les Bains.

Soon I was in the town square, La Place, where several tall white sycamore trees enhanced its peaceful feeling. I noticed people were eating in one of the two restaurants opposite each other. I found a small table at the first one, my back against its outside wall to face the town square. It was the perfect place to look more deeply at my experience on the Seat of Isis.

Called a "Pizzeria", the restaurant had many dinner choices, as it was now dinnertime. I wanted to have the French version of a pizza. It is served in a smaller size just for one person, that the French customarily eat with a knife and fork I noticed, watching.

My first bite melted in my mouth, as the sensuous pleasure of this moment took me to another experience of joy, different than that special moment on Isis's armchair. Suddenly, I had another memory of Isis sitting out in the cosmos when I took a shamanic journey into the upper world, just before I came to France this time.

She was sitting in a large armchair surrounded by what looked like pearls. I saw that each radiated a luminous essence, appearing as if it were its own world. I could see that in the middle where her chair was placed, the world above came to meet the world below as two Vs crossed and formed a diamond pyramid. I saw a beam of blue light come in and move along the walls of this diamond pyramid, and that if Isis was not momentarily there, her place would still be seen as a point of light.

She gave me a message:

It is the heart of the land calling you, calling for the return of the feminine, to remember and reactivate her ceremonies, to honor her again in her cyclic pattern. It was once done in the ancient times when this was a place of 'initiation'.

Momentarily, I carried her message in my heart as I placed the last bite of pizza in my mouth, slowly, because I was so full. It felt like I didn't have to eat for days. Then I got my bill and walked back to the hotel. Key in hand, I climbed the stairs to my blue room and was in bed asleep sooner than I'd ever anticipated, probably integrating Isis' messages on the higher planes, where it might be easier.

Again, it happened. I was riveted awake by something calling me at 4 AM. Visions were filling my head, while my body was sleepy, heavy. They kept coming. Perching myself up in bed, I reached for my pad to record it. There were no words, just pictures, telling some kind of story, like a song...if only I could hear it.

It was a different language, no words. Perhaps it was from beings in different dimensions, realities, or

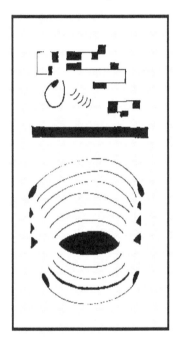

who were deep inside the earth here, trying to communicate to me. I drew everything, as best I could, fascinated by what appeared to be some kind of story. It was a different telling to what I was accustomed.

Hoping to understand more about these wordless teachings of inspiration, I later found writings from Catherine Gosh on *Sound* from the Integral Yoga Magazine, about the ancient scriptures from India that helped me facilitate answers:

The ancient primal traditions believed that the universe surrounding us sings to us...and that it is sonic in origin. Particular sonic 'codes' inform matter as to what it should look like on the outside, painting mystical pictures of a primordial sound from which the entire cosmos sprung. They see planets, stars and galaxies magically

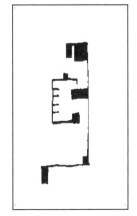

strung together by sonic frequencies. At an atomic level, everything is dancing and making its own music, vibrating at different sonic frequencies. The potential for sounds to affect us on a deep emotional level makes music our universal language, and according to ancient traditions, music is everywhere. We discover the power

of sound to transport us into the most delightful of destinations, divine locations we already contain within us, if we only let the music take us there. [5]

The next morning, hoping to calm myself from the previous days and nights full of such unusual mystical experiences, I chose to walk around the town in the morning, going nowhere specifically. Once again I walked over the bridge, looking down at the fish riding the currents in the clear waters, as a solitary person lay in the hot mineral bath.

When I walked by the building at the end of the bridge, there was a man working, so I said, "Bonjour." Then he walked over to greet me and started a conversation in French. He said they had recently purchased it and were making the building ready, along with another larger one, across the street, where people could stay. Then he summoned his wife in the next room. We greeted each other and then exchanged names. Hers was Rose.

Shorter than I, she had a smiling, pale, rosy face and light red-blond hair, her frame a little rounder than mine. Ready for a break, she walked me over to the other building they had finished renovating to show me some of the rooms.

Called "Les Angelos," The Angels, it was built up against the earthen hill, while the building on the bridge

"Maison du Pont," House on the Bridge was free standing. I admired them both.

Rose said she had planned to go for a drive to get away from her work, so she could be in nature. Spontaneously, she invited me to go. She said that a friend had recently shown her a mysterious saltwater spring high up in the hills nearby that was unusual. Wanting to share her intrigue, she invited me. I had mentioned my having to leave a few days later.

She drove. We passed through Rennes Les Bains, to a different bridge over where two rivers merged, La Blanque and La Sals, crossed it and headed to the source of this saltwater river, called *La Source Sale*. It was the same river that flowed in front of the hotel.

We passed wooded hills on both sides, and then passed through a tiny village where she turned onto a bumpy dirt incline. We twisted and turned on this narrow dirt road, when finally, at the top, it opened up to fields and a small stone farmhouse nestled off on one side. Rose found a spot to leave her car and we got out.

I walked behind her, on the dirt path shaded by sporadically placed trees. As soon as we had crossed a short wooden footbridge, I looked up to see a high ridge of vertical rocks on the edges of the field. They appeared in a semi circle, as if they were protecting something special.

We arrived at a simple, dirt opening in the earth, from which water was flowing out. It was unusually small. Rose said, "People consider this an enigma, having salt water come out of the earth so high up in the hills, and so far from the ocean. And no one has an answer for it yet."

Mesmerized by something, I found myself standing in front of it before I moved over to one side. Rose stood below me, looking out in the other direction, toward the farmhouse. I heard her sigh, one breath in and then she let it out. Her day had been filled with the anticipation of finishing their house project. I presumed she was tired.

And then it struck! Crack! Lightning! I felt it deep in my heart and was immediately aware of what the strike had done. It had brought up the water from deep within the earth, but salt water.

These lightning strikes happened right before my eyes…that is…the eyes of my inner vision. Quickly I remembered what Isis had told me, a day earlier, part of her story:

I said, NOW, and it began! With a bolt of lightning I seeded this place, as my light traveled down and marked places, sacred in these waters as I rested above.

In disbelief, I had to recognize how I had just stepped into a truth only revealed to me a day earlier. *Fast, that was fast*, I said to myself. I offered a prayer, acknowledging Isis as well as this sacred place, after which the skies opened up and the sun's rays seemed to reach out to touch my face. For a few long minutes, it embraced me with its warmth, before retreating back behind the clouds. It was a magical moment.

I thanked Rose for bringing me here, as we walked down to the car. Driving back to Rennes Les Bains, I knew this was the beginning of a long friendship.

When we arrived back at her house, I opened the car door, gathered my backpack and small water bottle. Reflecting for a moment, I asked if my proposed group in May could stay at Les Angelos. "Bien Sur " (Of Course), she replied, as we kissed each other on both sides of the cheek, the way they do in France. Then I returned to the hotel.

A day later it was time to get my things ready so I

could catch my return flight to Arizona.

Chapter 19 – Oak Creek Canyon

Back above the waters of Oak Creek in my tiny house, I hoped to have a day or two to adjust to the time difference. But no! I awoke the first morning at 4:00 am with more information from the Rennes Les Bains area. Again it was given to me in pictures.

Rubbing my eyes I tried to focus my attention before reaching for my trusty pad and pen. I had seen a room with two special Gothic shaped arches crossing over each other as I had seen my first visit to Rennes Les Bains. This time however I was being shown not only the box to draw but some kind of being with wings on top of it. I thought it was Isis.

Surrounding it I saw a green-colored six-pointed star and heard the words: *One has to walk through the six-pointed star to get to the Covenant.*

I assumed the voice was referring to the *Arc of the Covenant* as I soon saw a rectangular box with two tablet-like shapes on top. They were both blank.

Then non-stop symbols came to me so I drew the box from above, putting the symbols into the two blank tablets. Again it was an unfamiliar language. My hands moved continuously drawing these strange markings and then it was completed.

Later that day, wanting to look in more precisely I did a shamanic journey about the drawings and entered inside the mountain Pech Cardou, above the Little Cascade.

During this journey I saw designs on each side of the inner mountain passageway as I descended to where I arrived at a Gothic type arch and walked under it. I saw myself go through a green-color six-pointed star and then arrived at a rectangular box by itself with designs on the top of it, writings.

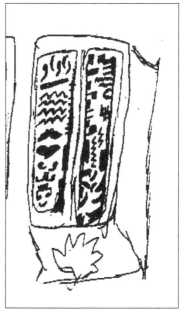

Once there I was aware of four white-robed beings standing around this box. An almond eye shape appeared, suspending itself horizontally, so I passed through it. Then I could see nothing more so I returned from the journey.

Mesmerized after receiving all these drawings, it seemed that indeed I was acquiring some kind of story about an inner place in the Rennes Les Bains area. Maybe there really was an ancient temple there.

After a day my inner clock recalibrated itself so my body returned to normal Arizona time and my sleep was uninterrupted. Now I was back to my physical life in Sedona and I had two more *Awaken the Magdalene Within,* sessions to complete before our nine month process was complete. Since the weather was still warm, we held one of them at my cottage in Oak Creek Canyon. It was early September.

Gathering on my stone terrace above the flowing waters of Oak Creek, Nicole arrived just before the eight women came down from Flagstaff. We were invited to share any realizations or situations that happened since our last meeting.

I shared my experience in France about the strong sexual energies while sitting outside a seemingly ancient temple doorway in Rennes Les Bains, after which my blood started flowing. Then I told them the story of how when it didn't stop after three weeks, I had to get help.

I mentioned receiving not only informational drawings from France but words spoken to me by some ancient beings, Isis, Magdalene, who seemed undoubtedly connected to the intention of our spiral, when I, at the beginning of it, had carried the intention to bring out hidden knowledge from the ancient Temple in France. In fact, during the later part of our gathering I hoped to introduce a temple ceremony shown to me by a "temple guide" in France, which Nicole invited me to activate with the group.

Curiously I received information as if I were being instructed to do a ceremony with others. The voice said: *Make a circle in the right place where you are surrounded by water to amplify the heart energy.*

Following these instructions we searched together to find the right place near my cottage and walked up closer to Munds Creek before it met Oak Creek. On a large flat rock partially covered by water, we all climbed down over the rocky bank, paying careful attention to where we put our feet. It was a perfect place.

Pulling out the white sage stick I'd stuffed in my backpack to cleanse everyone before tbhe ceremony, I lit it. As each woman stepped before me I moved the sage stick over her head, around both sides, her back, under her arms and feet. Then everyone was ready.

With our hands joined, we stood in silence in a circle waiting to see what might happen next. Then gently I felt my heart expand and noticed my friends Marlys, then Sheila, Karen, Bev and Nicole as our smiles broadened.

Then it began. We started vibrating together, gently at first then stronger and stronger. Nicole's smile was so expanded I could see her even rows of white teeth as her hazel/brown/green eyes sparkled. It seemed her face was laid over each of ours as she leaned backwards, our hands still engaged. Soon we too stretched our bodies backwards, like we had become a chalice together, waiting to be filled.

It felt like everyone's face had been laid over mine, no matter if she was tall, short, with a wide or narrow face. Suddenly we were united in one consciousness.

Wow, I said to myself, *is this really happening?*

Then I slipped into my other vision and suddenly saw that there was something that resembled a cone shape coming down from above. *No,* I said in disbelief, watching how it then connected with a cone that was coming up from below the earth. They were both the same size, maybe ten feet high and then met in the middle, where something unusual seemed to be laid down. It was a template and I saw it had coded symbols on it. *Amazing,* I thought.

We continued holding hands for a few more minutes until it seemed to be complete. I felt altered, in

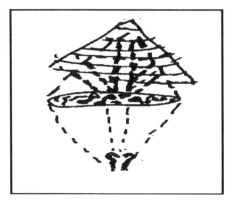

disbelief at what just happened. Some of my priestes sisters described vibrations they too felt.

Moreover, I was aware that this ceremony had been shown to me in Rennes Les Bains, while I was sitting in the Little

Cascade area. I drew these cones, remembering how the template spun in the middle as women, priestesses, surrounded it.

I was shown two snakes at the bottom of the lower cone facing each other, while a figure, the Mother Goddess I assumed was stationed nearby. Lastly, after completing the drawings I heard these words:

This is a place of remembering the cycles of the Earth and her energy swings as they relate to each season, as the wheels move consciousness. There is an ancient pattern of time and timing, that if we can remember the secrets that are hidden and preserved here, we can travel anywhere, know anything, feel and be anything, anyone, through the experience of 'Time Travel'.

Then the nearby feminine being, perhaps the mother goddess figure, wanted to identify herself:

I am the Goddess as old as time, spinning my wheels, my rhymes and rhythms of life. I am within, without, surrounding and that part which surrenders within. Remember me.

I who live here am all that is, was or ever will be. I am your mother, your daughter, your consort, yourself, your friend. I am all experiences, all pleasure, all sadness, all love and unrequited love. Reclaim who you are. Be reborn for who you want to be, always have been. Take off the veils.

We gathered our things and returned to my cottage where I ran to my tiny bedroom to get the drawings. I wanted to show everyone what had just been laid down before us, as most had not seen what I had.

Weeks later, approaching our final *Awakening the Magdalene Within* session, I wanted to review both Priestess processes, to assess how they were affecting my life. After my Emergence from the first nine month process I knew working with the Priestess, the Goddess mysteries was my new path, that I had been "called" and there was no going back. In fact as soon as the goddess had appeared to me down at the creek and invited me on an entirely new adventure, I followed her. She was presenting me with an infinite gateway.

It was as if I was waking up from some deep sleep; it was time to celebrate. Already I was beginning to feel like a different person, more refined in my life perception as I looked through my priestess eyes.

Furthermore, having Nicole or a facilitator's support while doing my inner search assisted me impeccably in re-discover my lost feminine qualities, my authenticity.

Lastly, as I approached my next ordination into the High Magdalene Mysteries, somehow it felt like it was time for me to step into another layer of my work. All the drawings and information given to me so far were part of it but I had no idea why.

Although I had claimed a lineage to Isis through Lady Olivia and carried Nicole's lineage forward, it was becoming obvious that maybe it wasn't necessary to be part of a lineage to be a Priestess. My true lineage was in my heart, carrying the wisdom in my own "walking temple". I was not greater than or separate from anyone else, except maybe my sensitivities were more opened than others. These processes had woken them all up.

During our Magdalene process we wrote a lot to bring up emotions from our subconscious. I liked doing this and will share one poetic piece:

The women are waiting most everywhere
For the Feminine Beings to descend from the air
They need harmony, balance and love within
But cannot end with just yin
The men too are yearning and spinning in
To access their Goddess and God self
And Begin
We have come here for union from a sacred time
That was once fulfilling and joyous
Not just a memory of mine
This sacred work clears all doubt away
Declaring inner union is here to stay
I am reaching and tugging for us to align
With our faraway stars
So blissful and sublime
We ask them now to play with us and shine
So we can all remember and anchor here
Such an incredible high
Oh my.

My *Ordination* was a small intimate ceremony in Flagstaff with just our group. The intentions I declared, as a Magdalene Priestess would carry what Nicole referred to as the High Magdalene Mysteries that after another year and a day would be sealed.

As I spoke my proclamation I faced my Priestess sisters and Nicole, declaring:

I AM Nancy Safford,
Magdalene Priestess of the Eternally Flowing
Heart Matrix of Sacred Union,
Through the Space -Time Continuum,
At the Point of Singularity
Where all Matter Originates
I Allow Myself To Be Guided
On Sacred Journeys around the World
To align 'her' energies with the land
In sacred re-union
So that it vibrates throughout the universe
In a harmonious balance
Of male and female polarities
To raise the Consciousness of All That Is
For The Highest Good
And so it is

Years later after reviewing this proclamation, I didn't question why I'd been given so much information about the inner temple in Rennes Les Bains. Surely I had called it forth. And there would be more.

Chapter 20 – In A Dark Robe

*L et Go...LET GO...*was being spoken into my ear, softly at first, then louder.

"Of what," I asked back. *Everything* was the reply. "I thought I had." *No, the house let it go.*

Facing the tall spires of Cathedral Rock, I had come back to sit in my favorite place, the place of "council" where the goddess figure first appeared to me years ago.

"No, no," I said to myself, "how can I do that...again?"

Months after my Magdalene ordination, I was working to stay grounded after receiving the many mysterious drawings about the inner temple in France. In fact, I was preparing to facilitate a group journey, myself, to France in two months.

Contemplating her words, I questioned how much further I could step into the *unknown*. Doing shamanic journeys into other realms was one thing, but putting my life, my physical life, into this unknown place again would be scary.

I was sitting on the dry spot of my favorite rock that was half immersed in the waters at Red Rock Crossing, weighing carefully every aspect of what her suggestion would entail.

I'd let go of everything when I left New York City at age twenty-two for Martha's Vineyard Island to do my first photographic book with just my cameras. After five years when it was published, I then let go of everything to live in France and document the French peasant farmers. For the next year and a half, I suspended any kind of personal life before returning to the US.

Now, after I had already 'let go' of my husband and home to focus on my emotions and deep feelings that had been stuck in hidden realms during the Magdalene process, I asked, "Where was I supposed to be going now?"

Shocked at my decision, wondering what part of me had made the choice, days later I decided to do exactly as she suggested. It took a month and a half of careful packing, storing my things in special places, after which I then passed my cottage to a friend who needed a small place, and departed. I had no idea where I would go after returning from France, but accepted that maybe this was an exercise from which I would learn something significant.

Departing for France to facilitate my own group, I arrived a week early. It was cool, the weather unpredictable this early in the season. We would be staying in Rennes Les Bains at my new friend Rose's B&B above the La Sals River. In fact my group was going to be the first one to stay at her newly renovated B&B.

I had reserved the apartment overlooking the River Sals and the high hills on the other side. With a living room, bedroom and kitchen, there was also a terrace and table outside for eating or being serenaded by the waters below. It was perfect for my group gatherings.

Most of the other rooms were simple and light, one or two beds, a sink and small closet, each with a window overlooking the river below. The building itself had been constructed against the steep hill long ago.

It was 1998 and I had organized that my group would be here to celebrate Beltane on May 1st, like in my Glastonbury experience. Not only about the fertilization of the Earth, this cross quarter festival was also about the harmonization of our own individual male and female energies within. To me it also seemed about awakening the "heart" that Isis and Magdalene had long ago imprinted, not only in the land here but in the sacred waters.

In fact it felt time to go beyond the endless stories and legends about the hidden treasures in the Rennes Le Chateau area. It was time to get back to the wisdom and spirit of the land itself, to the heart of the Feminine calling out to be replenished and honored, re-activated.

My first day, dressed warmly in short black boots, jeans and my warm quilted jacket, I turned right out the Les Angelos doorway, and headed straight for the Little Cascade. Excited to be here again, I turned down the narrow path, crossed the tiny bridge to the lower pond, and began, respectfully, saying prayers to honor the guardian Beings there, the unseen energies that had reached out to teach me things previously.

The day was cool as the sun sparkled on the water and reflected back a soft light. Moving cautiously to the water that flowed down into the lower pond, my feet moved onto a flat rock. I took out of my pack a small round, pale yellow crystal ball that I brought from Bolivia, and stood before the flowing cascade of warm water. While saying a prayer for my group journey, a white dove appeared out of nowhere and passed in front of me, from the right, to somewhere on the left.

Curiously, after finishing my prayer, the dove returned and squeezed itself through the tiny space between me, and the cascading waters, as if it were delivering me some special blessing.

Then I went back over the tiny footbridge, up the narrow path to the main street, crossed over the high bridge and then decided to walk along the River Sals to go upstream.

Navigating down a steep, unevenly worn stone stairway, I wanted to be next to the river. Although a wider, more common path was on the other side, this one I had never experienced. It followed the river upstream where at the first sharp curve, it narrowed into a barely discernible dirt path leading to the raised graveyard behind the church of Rennes Les Bains.

Fascinated by this new experience, I examined many ancient headstones, some shorter with rounded tops, trying to read the symbols on them erased by time. A few dated to the 1700s, then the 1800s, close to the newer headstones marked with the same family names, but more discernable.

Then I noticed a tall, thin unusually modern-looking black archway, unlike anything else in the graveyard, off by itself. It stood out so obviously that I went over to explore it. Mysteriously placed, it was a wonder who had built it and why.

I gazed down at the rich green grass surrounding it when all of a sudden it was like I had fallen down a long dark tunnel on some kind of journey. At the end of this tunnel was a group of beings, inside some kind of chamber walking in a tight circle. Each dressed in a dark robe with a hood, there were five or six of them moving together, possibly chanting. I couldn't identify if they had something placed in the center while doing what I assumed was some kind of ritual. It was eerie.

Suddenly realizing I was somewhere hidden from those in the physical world, watching something I probably shouldn't be seeing, I returned as fast as possible back up from the tunnel hoping my presence hadn't been noticed.

As fast as possible I crossed the graveyard to find the front door of the church, found the main street of Rennes Les Bains while noticing the restaurant in La Place where I ate on my last visit.

It was late in the afternoon when I arrived at my apartment and realized that soon it would be too dark to sit outside on my terrace, so I made an omelet, went over a few remaining details for my group coming in two days and went to bed.

Clunk! Violently, my bedroom balcony door was thrown open to jolt me awake. In the middle of the night, I awoke from a deep sleep. A dark shadowy figure had arrived in my room. As it came closer, I discerned a dark-robed figure.

As it moved over in front of me, I sat up, terrified, my back slammed against the headboard, huddled over as if I were a scared child. What had this dark being planned to do to me?

Facing me straight on, his eyes masked by a hood falling half over his face, he spit out his words: *We saw you watching us. No one knows what we do there and now I am going to RUIN you.*

His voice lingered on each word with a curse-ed declaration before he delivered his final words saying: *Just watch me STOP you!*

As he arched his hooded head toward me in his final long glance, I desperately asked myself, *Was he a vision or a real figure?* Then he turned to the outer terrace and disappeared through the balcony door. *Whack,* the door closed behind him.

Were his loud statements telepathic or from a human voice, I questioned? Either way, I got the message. Still terrified, I was immobilized. Frozen there for what seemed to be centuries within centuries, I slowly de-frosted and called for help from the higher realms: Mother Mary and Isis, Magdalene and Jesus, hoping they would help calm my wounded spirit. I knew the dark-robed being was definitely one of those I'd seen earlier in the graveyard performing some kind of ritual in that chamber under that dark-colored archway.

This situation brought up my early childhood and what had caused my fear of the dark, lasting into my mid twenties. I saw things I wanted to forget, nasty shapes moving around without form.

Waiting for the sun to come up that next morning seemed like waiting for a broken light bulb to turn itself on, the longest hours I'd ever remembered in a state like this.

At breakfast, I shared my encounter quietly with Rose who had never heard of anything similar happening here, but she hadn't been in the area long.

Moreover, I took the rest of the day to calm myself and to re-align with the intention for my groups' arrival, making a quick visit to the place where I did the prayers the previous day.

Chapter 21 – The Arrest

Anticipating my group's arrival, I checked each room Rose had reserved for us in Les Angelos, wanting everything to be comfortable for their first France experience. I placed small vases of pink roses in each room as a welcome.

They were from the southern state of Georgia, another place where Nicole had introduced the Priestess Process. Each woman on this trip was still in her nine-month process, as well as the one man, who had joined the men's Priest Process when Nicole introduced it for men as well.

Our small group would be staying in several different places around the area, and doing several simple ceremonies, marking this cyclic time from long ago. One place after leaving Rennes Les Bains would be in Rennes Le Chateau at the *Villa Bethanie,* on Beltane Eve before the building was declared a historic site when no one could stay there anymore.

Rose gave a warm welcome to everyone on their arrival, as we would be staying for the next three nights. The first morning we gathered in my apartment to initiate our journey, each setting his or her hopes and intentions. Then I introduced them to the nearby Little Cascade briefly, before I escorted them to a place where Alena had brought our group in 1996.

First mentioned in David Wood's book, *Genisis, The First Book of Revelations,* written in 1985, this site was referred to as *The Vagina of Nut,* a bold name for such a seemingly simple site. His research indicated how it involved the serpent, the egg and the womb, marked in the landscape here. His premise went back to Isis and ancient Egyptian mysteries.

The early peoples were aware of what occurred between heaven and earth, when cycles repeated themselves so they marked it for all to remember,[6] Wood writes. But who actually marked it, was still a mystery.

It was a few days before May 1st, when the seeds deep in the Earth were waking up and starting to grow again. Furthermore, I'd learned that Beltane was traditionally known as the time of the sacred marriage. The female represents the Earth while the male represents the spirit coming into the Earth, the manifesting into form, as it plants itself in the "womb" place. Interestingly the *Vagina of Nut* seemed an appropriate place to have our first ceremonial experience together.

Leaving Rennes Les Bains, I turned the car right so we could go on the other side of the mountain, Pech Cardou. Passing through the quiet village of Serres, onto a tiny road toward another village, Peyrolles, we arrived on top of a hill in a remote farming area. We got out and crossed over to a series of flat rocks down to a creek in the narrow valley below.

Without hesitation one woman quickly pointed out a circular, red dirt formation in the distance, high above the meandering stream. It was the most obvious formation in this mystical site. Dressed in her gold rain jacket, she stepped out and emphatically pointed her finger, "That looks like some kind of merry-go-round on the Earth," whereby she paused to reflect before continuing, "Do you think other kinds of Beings come and go from there?"

Amazed at her fascinating question-statement, I knew she was a "channel" and that people in Georgia came to her for insights into their lives. But I had no answers as we stepped down by the water, looking up at this "merry-go-round" rock. I learned that it represented "the egg" in the landscape, while our drive to it along the simple farm road was alluded to as being "the serpent", according to Woods in his book *Genisis.*

We positioned ourselves as I stood on one end while the others found their appropriate places next to each other. Opening up our ceremony, we called in the lineage of the feminine and other high beings to support us, including Jesus.

Quickly I sensed that a figure arrived to stand behind me and when I tuned in with my other vision, it seemed to be the Magdalene. At the other side of the group appeared another figure resembling Jesus. They seemed to be creating a structure of protection around us.

Sensing movement somewhere close by I glanced up at the circular red mound in the landscape on the high plateau. Something was happening that I'd never seen before or ever imagined seeing.

"Oh my God," I declared softly. Suddenly I was witnessing male figures in a Temple suspended above this mound, while women, feminine beings, appeared to be in a Temple beneath it. "Wow," I exclaimed again, as if it were some kind of mystical event being performed before my eyes when the Temple above shifted into the shape of a six-pointed star, a hexagon. But it was not done.

Next the women in their Temple quickly shifted into a pentagram shape, a five-pointed star. With the men above, the women below, each in their Temples, movement began between them. Somehow their points or facets came together, touched. And where they touched, tiny diamond pyramids were created. Then rainbows emanated from these points of contact.

"Oh my God," I exclaimed to the group, "This is like some kind of Disneyworld adventure." Then I asked to myself, *Is this really happening? What world are we in?* Questioning that these two different shapes could even come together to touch, I assumed that some important "event" was happening that defied all linear logic or reason.

Was it enabled because this was an ancient cross-quarter earth cycle or more likely, an important astrological alignment? No one had an answer. Although everyone wasn't able to see what I saw, they sensed something strong happening in their bodies, as the two Temples touched, then separated.

I questioned if we were solely watching it from the Temple Jesus and Magdalene had carefully formed around us or if we were participating in the actual ceremony. I wasn't sure.

My mind flashed back to my recent Magdalene ordination proclamation, realizing that I might have called this in when I declared myself:

> *Magdalene Priestess of the Eternally Flowing*
> *Heart Matrix of Sacred Union*
> *Through the Space-Time Continuum*
> *At the Point of Singularity*
> *Where All Matter Originates*

Looking at the last part of my proclamation, I had indeed declared:

> *I Allow Myself to be guided*
> *On Sacred Journeys Around the World*
> *To Align 'Her' Energies with the Land*
> *In Sacred Re-Union*
> *So That It Vibrates Throughout The Universe*
> *In a Harmonious Balance*
> *Of Male and Female Polarities*

To Raise The Consciousness Of
All That Is...For The Highest Good

Deep feelings began stirring in my physical body, as I realized we were indeed participants in this ceremony. It felt like I was receiving some kind of *transmission* after which I was informed by the beings who were overseeing this magical event that these two shapes, the hexagon and the pentagram, normally related to the solar plexus of the body. But interestingly, they alerted me they were shifting the "meeting place" in my body to be in my heart. Then it was over.

My priestess sister in the gold rain jacket bent down to touch the earth, offering her gratitude, while the others turned in different directions, their heads bent over in gratitude.

Rain began pouring down from the heavens, gently at first then harder, so we thanked all the Beings who supported us, Magdalene and Jesus, before hurrying back to the car.

Perfect I thought, it would be time to go to the bank so everyone could change their dollars into francs. It was years before the euro currency was in place. In fact I just changed my money here days earlier.

After parking my car across the street from the bank in the town of Quillan, we got out, walked over to the bank and entered. Since it was the end of the day, others had also come to make their last minute transactions, so I sat down to wait. My group found their places in one of the two lines in front of the tellers.

Realizing we were no longer in the "temple" with Magdalene and Jesus standing nearby, I focused on bringing my energy totally back into the present moment as I waited.

Then out of nowhere, a man came up to me. He asked me to follow him into his office. Wondering what was happening, I did. He identified himself as the bank manager as he sat down before me in his tan suit.

Maybe two minutes passed before a policeman entered, then another and another one, until there were five tall policemen standing there, somewhat idly, looking over at me. Curiously it felt as if I had committed some kind of bank crime and was someone they had to watch carefully.

The bank manager curtly informed me that the six one hundred dollar bills they had just changed for me, days earlier, were counterfeits. I realized that they had been waiting for me to come back into the bank so they could take some action against me. I explained that I got the dollar bills from my bank the same day I left Sedona, days earlier.

Then he informed me that these five policemen were going to follow me back to my Rennes Les Bains hotel, Les Angelos, in our two cars, so that I could repay the bank for the counterfeit hundred dollar bills.

Overwhelmed by my situation, I was embarrassed that it was happening in front of my group. My emotions went up and down, scared, wanting to cry in one moment and then feeling it would turn out alright, the next. But these deep emotions stuck like a lump in my throat.

Driving carefully, the police car behind me, I passed the ruined bath structures before entering Rennes Les Bains. As I approached the bridge to Rose's, turning left to cross it, something called my attention to look above me, employing my other vision.
I saw faces looking down on me from high above in fits of delirious laughter. They were the dark-robed beings. I could almost hear them laughing in some kind of eerie echoing way, that I imagined could spread out all over

the upper world, as they peered down at me in my dire situation.

It was as they had declared it would be. They were stopping me, trying to *ruin me*... my life.... and I feared it wasn't over yet. I watched them in the dimensions above my head, questioning how dimensions could be controlled like this, how their desires could be imposed so precisely in my physical reality?

After I parked my car, the policemen pulled theirs in behind mine to wait. I went in to get the money for them when Rose asked me what was happening as she glanced out at the police car behind mine.

Quickly I told her what happened whereby she bolted out her front door to speak to them directly. "This lady is not a criminal and she would never have planned anything like this, passing fraudulent monies." Then stating that she knew me well.

Coming down from my upstairs apartment I handed the six $100 bills to them, assuming the incident would be completed. Not so, I had to follow them back and meet the police chief who wanted to interrogate me.

Because this small town was located an hour from their main bank in the city of Perpignan on the Mediterranean, they were very careful. People arrived from many other countries, each having a different money system, he explained. Sometimes they were intentionally fraudulent.

Here I was face to face with the chief of police. Three people from my group sat nearby, supporting me with every ounce of healing energy, they later informed me. If I hadn't known French, I wonder what would have happened.

He asked me question after question, "Who were these people with me and what were they doing here? Was this a business situation or were they friends?

What was my business anyway and how did I make my money?" I responded, "Friends on a trip of exploration and I was a teacher," I explained.

My mind flashed on all the possibilities of what could happen to me. I could be arrested, I could be fined a great sum of money, I could be sent back to America. My heart beat faster and faster waiting for some reprieve, some relief that this tall pleasant-looking Frenchmen, seated before me in his dark blue police uniform, would declare as my fate.

I heard many cars pass on the main street outside his office, going to other destinations, some near, some far. I wished with all my heart I was in one of them, back in the normal world.

By his calm, cool, subtle manner of questioning me, it was obvious he was familiar with people who attempted to look normal, while underneath they were deviously trying to pull off some scheme using illegal tactics.

He continued to deliver questions and again I spoke my truth. The Sedona bank had made the mistake, not me; this had never happened to me, ever. I gave him my bank name and address so he could authenticate it as I sat there.

Minutes turned into what felt like hours, when finally, there was a faint gleam in his eye. The French chief of police had finally arrived at a decision. No, he decided, I was not an everyday criminal, traveling from country to country changing false bills into other currencies for my gain.

Emotionally worn out from worry and despair after he kept finding different angles to approach the same question, I was relieved when finally, he believed me. We were done. I was released. Lastly. I told him my next intention was to call my bank in Sedona and inform them what had happened.

As soon as I got to Rennes Les Bains I went into the phone booth and called them. After explaining my situation to a woman in the manager's office at Wells Fargo Bank and that, because of it I had just been arrested in France, I was shocked she had neither emotion nor compassion. In fact, I never received one apology from anyone there, ever.

When I returned to Sedona they repaid me and a lawyer helped me re-coop a small compensation for the situation it created. Yes, they replaced the false money given to me, but I realized my emotional stress could never be compensated, especially as it happened while I was facilitating a sacred journey for others. Immediately I took all my money out of Wells Fargo Bank and would never bank with them again.

Truthfully, I believed it was the dark-robed beings, who had mysteriously created this situation. Indeed there was nothing I could do about beings working from a hidden dimension. They had terrified me once and I hoped to never tangle with them again.

Chapter 22 – Lady With The Sword

For Beltane evening we would be staying at the *Villa Bethanie*, the only available place to stay in Rennes Le Chateau before it was declared a historic site and was then unavailable for visitors.

The Abbe Sauniere had constructed it at the turn of the century for "retired priests" he claimed, but after the extravagant parties and celebrations attended by famous out of town guests to whom he served expensive foods and high quality wines, the village people knew different.

We would also be celebrating, but our celebration would be focused on another perspective, one of earth's ongoing cycles. Our evening would be focused on the Goddess, the Feminine in a different kind of Priestesses duty, one of honoring Beltane, May 1st .

Above an ancient Temple of Isis deep in the Earth below, we were in a place of hidden identity. If Mary Magdalene had been an initiate in the Egyptian Isis Temples, she would be carrying that presence into the world, and to Rennes Le Chateau if she had truly been here, even if it was 2000 years ago. It is possibly why Sauniere had dedicated the two buildings to her, the church and Tour Magdala.

Staying one night in this most ancient place, we were each questing to find some mystery, either in the elusive village itself or one deep within ourselves. We were ready.

Everywhere we traveled on this journey, we left *despachos*, prayer offerings introduced to me a year previously in Peru by my Peruvian shaman teacher. These were offerings to the spirits of the land, the mountains or to the waters that allowed a Peruvian person, often a shaman, to pass over a mountain or cross a waterway with reverence.

Despachos were like tickets so the person or people who created them could step beyond the place they were, literally or figuratively in which specific items were placed. Often included in it were cords of gold and silver, representing the sun and the moon, possibly crystals, holy water or other cleansing liquids, maybe food items that had a specific significance. Our *despachos* however, were a little different than those of Peru.

Including the gold and silver threads, we added other significant items, maybe a slice of apple representing the fruit of life, flowers for the beauty of life, cake or something sweet for the sweetness of life. Sometimes we poured wine over the top or sacred waters from the many springs that carried codes of the universe. When completed it would be closed, then wrapped, ready to be either buried in the earth or burned to release its blessings.

When we arrived on the holy hilltop of Rennes Le Chateau, it was late afternoon. My car had woven around the many turns on the snake-like ascending path to get us here before I parked in the lot overlooking the valley. We each gathered our suitcase and coat, ready to check into the *Villa Bethanie*.

The room keys were with a man, Jean-Luc, who ran the garden restaurant next to the Villa Bethanie, as well as the Villa Bethanie hotel itself. Pleasant scents were emanating from his outside grill as I went to collect the keys from him.

We had the only rooms on the second floor with two more available on the third floor where guests could also stay if there was need. Legends said that many had experienced comfort here for decades.

The ground floor had a tile floor laid with beautifully interwoven geometric patterns in muted reds, grays and white. Its elegance was an extreme contrast to the hardened dirt floors that most of the Rennes Le Chateau's villagers had in their homes at the turn of the century, I later learned. It was no mistake why Sauniere's reputation traveled so far and wide, carrying details of this luxurious building.

Two rooms were in the front of the tall square-ish building, each with a window facing the street in front, one on each side of the creaky winding staircase that brought an eerie spin to our stay here each time we used the stairs. I would be sharing a room with my priestess friend who wore the gold rain jacket.

The path outside the front door sloped downward toward the Magdalene church. If we turned right, we stepped onto the part of the path that ascended, leading to the Tour Magdala. Interestingly, the *Villa Bethanie* was situated between two places dedicated to Mary Magdalene.

Laying my suitcase on the bed, I felt a heaviness floating in the room that lightened when I moved to the center. Clinging to the walls near my bed, it was as if a heavy cloud were carrying stories from long gone parties no one cared about today.

They weren't divulging information about hidden mysteries here, but instead might possibly be carrying unresolved emotions released after a guest had sampled one too many aperitifs or enjoyed too much rich wine. I was glad to have reserved only a night for my group; two might have been one too many.

Instinctively, I moved my bed several inches from the wall and Jeannie my roommate did the same, as she too was sensitive to these moving fields of emotions.

After depositing our belongings, we walked carefully down the once elegant stairs that in their sharp semi-circular design brought us to the bottom to a delicately carved oak door. We could turn to the old dining room on the right or to the parlor on the left, but we continued straight ahead, down four steps to the entrance door, and went outside.

Together we walked under the tower of the Tour Magdala, as it protruded over the edge of the hill. I stopped to rest my back against the side just below the curve of the Tour, while the rest of the group turned right and found places to stand in front of it.

The sun warmed my face on this cool day as the calmness brought a sense of peace that enveloped my heart. But then unexpectedly, something appeared, as if it were stepping out of some other dimension, and my *other vision* took over. Two rows of Priest-type beings dressed in white robes arrived and stood before me in a semi-circle. They looked like they could have been Templars or members of some *high councils* possibly even members of the *White Brotherhood*. They faced me to speak, as if we were all standing in the same world:

We have been holding the energy here for so long, we now propose that it is time for the feminine to take it back, for the feminine to get back in the center. The time of the patriarchy is changing, they said, before they added their final words, *And we have done well to keep secret all that we have here.*

Still within my deep vision, I looked below the Tour Magdala where I had seen a circular area surrounded by water once before. Yes, I saw that it was still visible, but this time there was something I hadn't seen then, something more. There was a female figure standing in the middle of the area, in a temple. I gasped, realizing that she was a Goddess, a Priestess figure still holding her space in the temple, possibly waiting for something, someone.

Oh My God, I said to myself remembering a year previous when I'd made a quick visit to France and come to Rennes Le Chateau. Standing in the same place, I'd seen a temple below. Belonging to a Goddess, a Priestess figure, who had spoken to me then, she said:

The feminine energy was here long before the masculine energy and this is a place where the feminine energy comes to the Earth, to anchor and communicate with the feminine star system.

Immediately I received images of this temple that began as a circle with a smaller circle within it. A cross originated and extended out from the center of the smaller circle, touching the four directions on it before meeting the larger circle's edges and touching it in four directional points. At each point it touched I had seen a temple. After I saw this, the Goddess, Priestess continued speaking to me, saying:

Each place represents a specific star system or planet and at different times of the year certain information was brought in here.

Then she was finished. My attention returned to the beings standing in the white robes before me who were trying to show me how they appeared here daily, in a "routine" which involved walking down the narrow path in front of the Tour Magdala, as far as it took them, in a manner that seemed almost "ritualistic". *Were they weaving a protective web around some ancient lineage or wisdom stored deep in the Earth* here, I questioned? Their steadfast mission was admirable for however long it had been happening. I hoped we could one day uncover the ancient knowledge that had been stored here.

Shortly after I walked over to where my group was, just past the Tour Magdala. We decided to take turns watching each other, one by one, to identify any unusual effects appearing around someone's head or body. Each stood against the stone foundation next to the Tour Magdala, looking out.

I remember seeing amazing things happen with Jeannie's aura, as she sat braced between two tall vertical grey rocks, as colors surrounded her head, pale pinks and greens, light blues and then purples that morphed together into tiny light particles. As the subdued colors mingled together, she said she felt an ecstasy. Each person's experience was different.

When we finished, I glanced over at the place people refer to as the *Magdalene Cave*, opposite the Tour Magdala. It was hidden inside the limestone cliff above the river. I looked at its dark vertical opening and was suddenly greeted by a tall figure I assumed was Mary Magdalene. *This was a place of teaching,* I heard, and quickly flashed on the cave lit up with candles in a circle, when she continued to say: *A teaching and initiation are in process, in this Mystery School,* before she was silent.

This was my first indication about actual teaching being done here, and especially by Mary Magdalene herself. I questioned what the teachings would have been about, the earth and our celestial heavens, or ceremonies and priestess training? Maybe they were about the wisdom related to our feminine ancestors who might have come in here from the stars. I imagined it was an intricate part of the temple I had drawn beneath Rennes Le Chateau. Like a puzzle, there were so many pieces to put together so the bigger story could be revealed and understood.

Suddenly feeling that the temperature had dropped, we, my group, walked over to Jean-Luc's garden restaurant to choose from his grilled meats and vegetables for an early dinner.

Later, on the eve of Beltane, we gathered in one of the bedrooms, the one larger than any of the others that could hold all of us. Plus it was too cold outside now to do a ceremony.

Sitting in the middle of their large bed, we each found our spot. Mine faced an elegant turn of the century window with wavy old panes; I noticed several had been replaced by new clear glass.

Ready to begin our Beltane ceremony, we, the priestesses, formed the inner circle, while the one Priest held the space on the outer perimeter. By joining our hands and being still, our hearts connected as we began to engage the male and female energies. I called in the *heart matrix of sacred union* after which others added their words, as we honored the sacred moment when opposites unite.

One woman took her hand and wiped sweat off her brow, saying, "Wow, do you all feel this heat?" I agreed knowing that my body also was very hot and I moved off the bed and stood up so my body could cool down. Together we released the energies and beings that had assisted us, before closing our ceremony.

Knowing that the male/female energies had been honorably anchored at Rennes Le Chateau, our Beltane mission was complete. We said "Goodnight" to each another and went to our rooms for bed.

Back in the room, I was fully energized, questioning if sleep was even possible. I had brought along several items, including gold and silver threads, fruit, sacred water that I always carried with me and a few other things, along with a biodegradable wrapping, a simple napkin.

Then I asked Jeannie, who was sitting up in bed with a gleam in her eye, "Would you be willing to sneak down with me, at midnight, the true Beltane moment, and bury a *despacho* in front of the Tour Magdala?" We discussed how it would be cold, probably eerie and a little scary, but it wasn't long before she said, "Yes" to the adventure. We had already claimed a few significant experiences in one short day and were curious what might be next.

We dozed off waiting for the midnight hour, but it was Jeannie who quickly got up minutes before midnight and declared: "It's time." Partially dressed already, I slipped into my jeans, pulled my sweater over my head and slipped into my black boots. Angling my favorite beret on my head, I reached for my jacket. Jeannie was bundled up the most I'd seen her, in her light brown woolen coat and wearing her beige woolen hat. We were ready.

After gathering the *despacho* items, I found my little flashlight so we could carefully descend the staircase without any disasters. With not a sound from either of the other rooms, this would be our midnight adventure.

Down the eerie staircase of the Villa Bethany, we stepped slowly and carefully along the dark wood paneled staircase. We made a few creaks now and then as we proceeded to the door at the bottom. Together we opened it.

As soon as I stepped outside my cheeks were smacked by the cold air and released any embers of warmth still lingering there. We turned and walked the incline to the Tour Magdala.

Silence, not one sound was audible, nothing. All the birds were nested in their warm hideaways, leaving an element of magic hanging in the air as the night stars sparkled far above us.

In my one hand I carried a flashlight, in the other a bundle of items closely assembled for our *despacho.* Jeannie carried a soupspoon for digging the hole and a few more items for our prayer offering to the spirits at Rennes Le Chateau.

Approaching the mystically tall building at this hour, side by side, Jeannie and I turned around the corner under the spiraling tower of the Tour Magdala. It seemed like it was reaching endlessly through layers of heavens in a never-ending journey to somewhere unknown.

To the left of the Tour Magdala, we searched for a place to dig the hole and chose a place where the Earth and solid rock wall met, the wall curving slightly. I set my objects on the ground as Jeannie tried to dig out the hard dirt. It was stubbornly solid, but shallower than we intended, when finally we decided to lay down the soft napkin and fill it with the designated offerings. One after the other we stated what each represented, our teeth chattering by the end.

The moment Jeannie scooped the last bit of soil over our *despacho* and had stepped aside, the winds picked up suddenly as a big swooshing sound circled around us. It was as if we had just deposited something into the great abyss, not just any abyss, it was the one connected to Rennes Le Chateau.

No, I said to myself when I recognized that the Priests in the white robes had created this big swooshing sound, the ones who spoke to me earlier. They were arriving to accept our gift and all the prayers it held. I could see them gathering around it with my other vision

Unusually disturbed by these energies, Jeannie quickly ran off further down the path. Minutes later she returned. Then together we moved over underneath the

Tour Magdala, facing it side by side. She was on my left.

Not more than three minutes later my jaw dropped open, wide. Another swooshing sound, but it was not the white-robed priests. I was gazing up at a very tall unmistakable female form maybe 20 feet tall, standing in front of me peering down.

She had quickly and quietly appeared, as if she had been waiting inside the Tour Magdala since the beginning of time. But now it felt like she wanted to speak. She was ready to be heard. She carried a long sword in her hand proportionate to her tall stature. I thought immediately that it was Mary Magdalene and didn't question who else it might be, not until years later.

The sword glistened in her hand as she angled it carefully, waiting to proceed. I couldn't discern if I could reach my hand out and touch her form or if it had a physical substance, because she seemed to engage me in another reality. I had no recollection of details such as the color of her eyes, what clothes she was wearing, if there were edges to her form, or if she had any semblance of being human, as we knew *human* to be.

She was real to me in this moment and I was ready to listen. I felt that she had something specific to ask me. After a long silence, her voice was distant, like an echo that seemed to come to me through some faraway place. She began, asking simply:

Will You Do My Story?

Both stunned and shocked at her request, my response was immediate. Without thinking or wondering at length if I could do it or why I couldn't, out of my mouth came my response,

Yes, I Will!

But I was ready to scream out in fear when she swung her long sword up and held it above me. Close, she brought it close, touching my right shoulder with the broad flat blade, softly. Then she moved it over to touch my left shoulder doing the same thing, even more softly. It felt as if I were suspended in some kind of time warp when she made her final gesture by touching my head more firmly with the almighty blade of her sword.

My body was tingling. It appeared that I was being *knighted,* although perhaps there was a more ancient ceremonial meaning to what she was doing. Moving the sword back in front of her, she held the top with both hands. I felt her gaze on me for some seconds, possibly watching my energy field. Seeming that her *mission* was complete, she turned to leave.

I watched her depart. What appeared to be wings were behind her. As she traveled farther away, I could see that she was traveling in a *diamond of light.* Before she was totally gone from view, I saw an almond-shaped symbol, also called a vesica pisces, close behind her, like it was an outer doorway, a portal through which she had arrived.

Still standing there, once again, I found myself staring into where she had been. Nothing remained. I turned to Jeannie, never inquiring about her experience because I was still lost in my own and still speechless. We left, going around the corner of the Tour Magdala down to open the doorway of the Villa Bethanie. Closing the inner door, we climbed as quietly as possible up the dark stairs, without one creak.

Without a word we each slipped into our warm nightgowns and retreated to our beds under the covers, each dwelling in our own individual story. I would think about *Her Story* another day.

Chapter 23 – The Healing

After dropping my group at the Toulouse airport for their flights, I returned to Rennes Les Bains, ready to establish peace within myself, before returning to Sedona days later.

Exhausted from all the stress and penned up emotions that hadn't been fully released, my body needed healing from the two shattering situations that happened, first the one before they arrived and then the one in the bank during my group, with them witnessing it.

Now I wanted to sit in my favorite place on Mt. Bugarach where I could find council with the earth there, where I had begun a relationship. Mt. Bugarach was often covered in clouds that hid its peak daily. Magically it lent a certain presence to the landscape, being there one moment, then gone the next.

Geologists claimed Mt Bugarach was upside down, making the part above, visible at the summit, older than what was in the earth below it. Interestingly, over a hundred caves have been found inside, research says, where different groups of people once lived, possibly the Essenes, then later the Cathars who performed many of their initiations in caves.

Several paths lead up to the top of Mt. Bugarach but the most popular one is on the left side as you face the mountain. After traversing back and forth on the narrow winding road, higher and higher, I found the small parking area on an incline and left my car.

Hiking to the top can be strenuous and take several hours, depending on your physical condition, but my favorite spot was only a twenty-minute climb. I was excited to be making this short but steep hike next to a luscious green pasture, where a few white cows were grazing in their peaceful worlds. I turned off to my special path and arrived at a wire fence, which I ducked under. It led to a small meadow, thick with clumps of grass-covered rocks I had to either walk around or climb over.

At last, there it was - I found the elongated rock. Climbing up onto the sunken area in the middle, this was "my seat". Here I could catch my breath from my non-stop climb, as I sat down in the hallowed place. *Whew,* I said to myself, *I made it.*

As my body relaxed, my heart began feeling at home in the calming energy from the mountain. I was ready to finally release the emotions my body and spirit had been holding, ever since my arrest in the French bank and after that eerie dark-robed figure had cursed me.

My eyes closed, perched on my favorite seat, I felt good. I wished it were a celestial throne where idealistically nothing could or would ever bother me again. Slowly drifting off, I heard a faint voice speak to me, saying:

Are you ready now for the time of your life? This is the Magdalene speaking. Reach out and let me embrace you. It is time to open the cathedrals of your heart to find the peace, harmony and beauty of life that you have been waiting for.

I heard myself respond, asking: "Will it be hard, or painful, necessary to process a lot?"

No, this is the new reality we are embracing, where heaven and Earth shall merge. We shall re-emerge to renew our pact together.

I quickly asked: "Have we known each other before?" She answered:

Yes, don't you remember? Look into those lost places within and you will find me. Empower your fears, your shadow so you can be free! That's why we're here you know, to free ourselves from the past, from all the pain, wondering, am I right, am I wrong, am I happy, will I be fulfilled, will I know joy and beauty? I am here to lead you on the greatest journey of your life... the one to yourself. Join me now on the journey of remembering.

I come from the depths of the cosmos, where your heart harbors the depths of your passion. It is here you will find me. Lead me to the place of desire, because I am beyond that, beyond all definition. Remember me.

Whew! I released a big breath staring out at the green hilly landscape below. Diminished, my anxiety and heavy heart relaxed, I felt freer. *Yes*! I exclaimed to the world from my mighty seat as I sat a little longer, before thanking Mary Magdalene for her loving, timeless message. I got up to leave.

It was as if I was flying with a new sense of freedom, as I descended the hill and slid into the car with as much grace as possible, recognizing how I was more at peace with myself than when I arrived.

Chapter 24 – Attachments

I had no place to live. That feminine voice told me to *Let Go,* so I did! As soon as the bank reimbursed me for the fraudulent money they had given me, I "let go" of the bank too. Where was I now?

My decision was to leave Sedona and move outside to a calmer place, integrating what had happened recently in France. Literally I needed some distance.

In Cornville, a small farming town twenty minutes south of Sedona, I found a house share. Down a small country road called *Purple Sage,* I had a room with a balcony looking out to distant mountains; it was time to slow down and find stability on a more daily basis.

My bedroom and small living space were perfect, although most of my time was spent at a small table on the balcony writing details from my recent three year shamanic training session or enjoying the late May weather.

Prompted by a need to make money, I soon applied and was hired by a well-known Sedona jeep company to do spiritual tours, which included vortex experiences and medicine wheel ceremonies.

It felt empowering to learn how a four-wheel drive vehicle could climb over and then down between large rocks that no normal car should ever attempt. Learning this crafty driving was a Sedona adventure in itself. Because I had many fears, it took more than two weeks of instruction and every day practice before I was ready to take others out.

A few months later I met a man whom I avoided at first. I had a strong vision of him from an earlier time, a past life, where he appeared as a rather sinister, almost magician-like person with slightly hunched shoulders, standing in a large room, a temple, possibly in Atlantis.

As my remembrance continued, someone had brought me to meet him, to possibly assist him with a project he was designing. In this vision I remember distinctly the way he looked up at me from his worktable, sizing me up. Seeming to be a cold person lost in his work, as soon as he learned about my expertise with lasers he wanted me to work with him. I was not sure however, if he was working with the light or the dark. I never looked in to see more.

His appearance was different now. Handsome, he had brown sparkling eyes and dark peppered hair he sometimes tied into a ponytail. His voice had a special tone to it, musical, that could soften any heart, including mine. He was called Jason.

One day he invited me on a walk with him and I accepted. He had a dog, Bear, a brownish-orange colored chow, who, if he liked you, was happy to walk next to you, but if not he chose his own way. He was very discerning. Since I loved animals, especially dogs, we established a good relationship, he liked me and I him.

We took a few more walks, some outside of Sedona to places he often went with Bear, exploring Sedona's Oak Creek or the forest higher up in Flagstaff. He had a small seventeen foot trailer he hauled behind his truck, spending weeks at a time away from the everyday world.

One time I found him down a road outside Sedona where he'd set up his easel and was making visionary drawings. He was connected to a very creative source, as I watched him complete one and go right on to draw a second, then a third, each very different from the last.

A week later he invited me for dinner at his studio apartment. We ate simply, pasta, but laughed and joked a lot, before I got up to leave. It was late and I had to drive back to Cornville. After embracing warmly I found myself still there in the morning. Some kind of relationship had begun.

Creating fountains, I soon learned, was also something Jason did well. After seeing a few he showed me with water flowing over purple amethyst crystals or varying sized pink and clear quartz crystals, I could see how they brought not only beauty to an environment, but that they enhanced its overall feeling.

Evidently, he once channeled archangel Metatron before I knew him, the highest angel of light, but stopped after becoming more interested in *enlightenment* and *satsang* teachings from the lineages and gurus from India.

Then several *enlightened beings* who were believed to be carrying the presence of enlightenment into their everyday lives began visiting Sedona, offering these *satsangs*. During my first experience, I watched as individuals went up to sit with him or her, asking questions about truth and how to be in the present moment. Sometimes it would elicit an answer, but more often the *guru* offered a *transmission* to them without words, a direct experience of presence they hopefully would not forget. Then another person would go sit next to the guru and the evening continued like that.

It was an entirely new experience for me and gave me a new perception of life, briefly, of how one could live it with *detachment*. I saw that it was what life could be, realizing that, *maybe this was where all my 'letting go' was supposed to lead me.*

Having desires indicated that one was embracing a "doing" mode, aspiring "to get" something that was not in the *present* moment. It could include aspects of attachment to physical love or to making lots of money from the *desire* to have things in the physical world, like nice cars and fancy homes. The physical world was seen as being an *illusionary world* or *maya,* which seemed not very different from the Cathar beliefs in southern France.

Furthermore, this belief was the opposite of everything I, we, had been brought up to believe in America, aspiring toward "the American Dream." It encompassed all things money could buy.

But I liked the feeling of these *satsangs*, because my heart felt expanded, light, full of joy. I had to admit, however, that my experiences aligning with my Feminine guides and teachers, Mary Magdalene, Isis, and other voices that had no names, gave me similar feelings.

Soon everyone in Sedona was talking about *enlightenment* and how to achieve it. However in this teaching I learned there were two routes, either the direct route, which was a one on one with your source, a solitary path or the second, where you brought the consciousness out into the world for others, like many gurus in India were doing, many women, like Amma, even Mother Mary from long ago. It seemed they wouldn't rest until all beings had achieved enlightenment, their own connection to the divine.

Then Jason met a woman attending one of these *satsangs* who called herself a *guru,* and said she assisted people to become *enlightened.* In fact she had created a living situation in her home, calling it an *ashram,* so people could experience living a daily life from this teaching.

Realizing that Jason was focused on enlightenment, she invited him to live there. Because we were in relationship, I was invited too. Three hours east of Sedona, her house was near the White Mountains, Show Low, and interestingly close to land I had bought years ago when Robert and I were married.

Because he was anxious to go, I, with a blind sense of trust, quit my jeep job and followed him in this new adventure. Unsure of where it would lead me, I recognized the unstable financial future it could present.

For the moment, I also let go of actively following the Feminine path, the Priestess and leading trips to France. Furthermore I was still feeling unsure of that dark-robed figure in France, unsure of where we might meet again and what the figure could do to stop me from doing "my work" there.

When we arrived at her *ashram,* Jason and I were separated, he in his room, me in mine. Shocked it was already happening, my true teaching of *detachment.* I was not meant to have any desires now.

Emotions began to surface for me, as I was trying to define love in a personal relationship. Not only based on what I had already experienced in my life, it was from the perspective of the Magdalene work I'd done of reclaiming my lost sexuality, discerning the sacred from the profane and then exploring the difference between the physical and spiritual experiences of love.

Thus, my question in discerning between these teachings was about my choice now. What did I want in my life? Disturbingly, I was torn by the possibility of losing Jason to an ancient teaching, a belief, whereby having a relationship was not important, not as I knew it. So yes, *I had attachments.*

Two weeks passed. Jason wanted to leave. It seemed something between them, as I sensed our *guru* wanted him as part of her ashram, to possibly work *with* her. He was often in blissful, joyful states possibly demonstrating early stages of *enlightenment*. But she wouldn't allow Bear inside her house. He had to sleep outside in the trailer. Jason hated this, which possibly was a deciding factor. Was it because Bear was an *attachment* or that she didn't like animals? I never knew. Now the question was, *Where would we go from here*?

Interestingly, the cheap land that I bought during my marriage to Robert was nearby. At the time many others from Sedona rushed over to buy their parcels too, some going in together to have a forty-acre parcel. Excited, I bought mine thinking I'd one day spend time out there, maybe even have a small cabin.

We decided to go there, live in his trailer; that way Bear could be part of our experience. It was a triangular forty-acre piece of land that I fenced after people stated cutting the juniper trees for firewood. I put in two gates, one along the common dirt road a mile from the main road, the other on the front side of the property facing the White Mountains in the distance. I preferred this one.

We turned off the main road twenty miles east from the Mormon town of Snowflake and drove a mile down the bumpy dirt road to the gate facing the White Mountains. Naturally the gate was locked, so after finding my key, I opened it. Jason turned his truck in with the trailer behind, and, I, after closing the gate, followed in my car.

Unexpectedly, at this exact moment a little voice spoke up from inside me, with trepidation, asking, *What are you doing?* So I reflected on it briefly then answered to myself, *Yes it's another adventure, but maybe I'll learn about living on the land, because I've never done anything like this before. Maybe living a simple life can bring me to a deeper understanding of the spiritual realms. And this is a way for me experience being on my land, because I'm with someone who knows about these things.*

Shaggy bark juniper trees in varying twisted shapes covered the property. It was high desert land, barren, without one patch of rich brown dirt. The winds had pushed the sand around making high dune like mounds, similar to being on a beach in a few spots, but without the ocean water.

Searching for the right place to put the trailer, we chose a protected spot, near several larger juniper trees. Small, the trailer was efficient, with a tiny shower, a double bed, a couch stretching the width of the trailer in the back, a sink and a gas burner area for cooking, with a few cupboards for dishes. It was a lot compacted into one tiny seventeen foot trailer. I was happy to have the fencing around the property, it made it more private, safer too if I was ever alone.

The nearest store where we could pump our water was twelve miles from the land. Jason knew the details from his many trailer experiences and had several 5 gallon jugs. Thus, we began "hauling" our water. It was for having quick showers, cooking, drinking, washing clothes and for whatever else we had to do. It went fast I soon noticed, making this a twice a week chore.

Bringing comfort to our outdoor living situation occupied Jason now, when, not more than two weeks after we arrived, he found two big armchairs at a nearby garage sale. He placed them outside the trailer and covered the area with a thick tarp roof so we could sit out of the sun. Our previous arrangement was plastic chairs from which we watched the stars at night. I liked our new arrangement.

On my daily walks to the outdoor toilet in an alcove of trees, I gained a new confidence and understanding about the land and the animals sharing it, from snakes and rabbits, to coyotes and occasional rats whose nests were in some of the more distant trees.

Living out here was a new adventure for me, as far away from walking down a crowded New York City street as you could get. We had no agenda, nothing to do here. Each day we would get up, heat water on the tiny burner for tea or coffee and discuss what might be next. Sometimes on hotter days, after washing my face and dressing in the coolest clothes I had, shorts and a sleeveless shirt, I'd take a walk around the property for exercise with Bear by my side.

Crazy with laughter, I loved when Jason danced to music on our cassette player. He would make short directional moves with his body, forward, than backward, arms up and down, in front and behind him, always glancing over to see my face. He loved to amuse me when he could, lightening me up when I got too serious or worried out there. His dancing was to make me laugh, and I always bent over laughing. It softened our relations, too.

Graciously the forest service gave us permission to gather the logs they'd cut down or that had fallen and been left idle in the forests nearby. After we hauled them back, Jason constructed an outer wall in front our living area. He made a rustic ceiling with them and attached thick plastic from it that came down and became our front window. He laid a crude floor using other old boards that helped separate us from always stepping on the compacted sand, improving our primitive living condition.

One day, months after our arrival, we found a stray dog in the nearby town and brought her home. Pepper, we called her, as she was a black and white Australian Sheppard mix. When she quickly came into heat, Bear mated with her. We kept two of the puppies, Brahman and Yogi.

I liked having the dogs; my favorite part of the day was when we all went for our evening walk together, exploring views from different spots on the property.

Jason began creating unusual experiences when he designed a pyramid structure not far from the trailer, using metal rods. He put a chair at the center so people could enjoy an uplifting experience, but one neighbor, in clear view of it, became fearful of what we were doing. These were not the same people as in Sedona.

Soon after Jason realized that his dream was to have a place, land, where people could come and find peace. It would be like a community, whereby people could assist with necessary work. It seemed an offshoot of the ashram where we had been briefly.

I was still connected to my guides and teachers and would sometimes do shamanic journeys to keep my visions clear. Most significant for me however, was the special altar I created at the foot of a cluster of juniper trees, where I would sit daily to connect with some of my guides and teachers.

I remembered the agreement I'd made with that tall lady with the sword, Magdalene I thought, who stood before me on that cold midnight in front of the Tour Magdala. But I hadn't kept my agreement yet and questioned if she would come searching for me.

A year had passed and we had created an experience of living off the grid, with solar power and a back-up generator for electricity. It was a simple, almost primitive living arrangement. Many people on nearby plots of land were on welfare, which for the first time gave me a glimpse of how it takes care of people who have less, who find themselves in compromised living situations.

Seeing them sometimes in the grocery store, I realized they might never get out of it their situation – or sadly – *could never* get out of it and go back to a life closer to their dreams. But then it occurred to me, *Maybe they have no dreams*. But I assured myself, *I did.*

Assessing my situation more seriously, I began questioning what was ahead for me. Basically I hadn't much money. I let go of everything to be here, my friends, clients in Sedona who brought financial support, a jeep tour job, my Priestess work facilitating groups for others, doing France journeys, and even an offer to work as a photographer for the famous *Arizona Highways Magazine*.

Jason had no designs on getting any kind of job, as his philosophy was about being detached. Sometimes he sold his crystals at nearby flea markets. Because I had some credit card bills from my spending extravagances during my marriage, I found a weekend job and started traveling back and forth to Sedona.

Every possession I had was stored in a second trailer someone gave us when they sold their parcel. After cleaning and painting it, we put our belongings inside. After emptying my Sedona storage unit, I brought everything out to the land just to save money, but I did it with a mysterious trepidation.

Not long after, our relationship began to change, whereby some days we got along and on others we didn't. We were in a tight living space, always in each others' energies whether we wanted it that way or not. I began noticing that it seemed there was strange energy coming through him, targeting me.

Curiously while sleeping next to him, these energies seemed to be reaching over to attack me. Thus I tried to protect myself by putting one or two of his powerful laser crystals between us after he fell asleep. It helped for a while.

Then I found myself caught in a past life memory with him. One evening while we were making love together, I felt snakes moving inside my stomach and it made me so sick I needed to disengage.

Looking in further, I discovered that it was a Roman past life when he had picked me up from the streets as a very young woman. Maybe my family had died and I was bereft. In that lifetime he waited until I got older and then forced me into sexual situations, thinking he *owned* me, which might have been common in those days. Unmistakably I felt suddenly stuck in this long ago memory.

To disengage totally from it, I moved out to a little trailer another friend had recently given us, when she too left her land, not ready for a life like we had. Placed nearby under a small cluster of trees, I carried some things over and made up the bed. Jason didn't make a big issue about it because he seemed to know that our relationship was changing. He knew I had some past life issues coming up.

Then other situations came up, as if some hidden doorway had just been unlocked. I was face to face with memories from my childhood when my mother began doing unusual things that terrified me. This fear touched on a feeling that something or someone "unseen" was after me, out to "get me" and so I wouldn't be alone in the dark then.

Now it was my subconscious mind still seeming to hold the imprint of something I had to look at and address. Whatever was coming through Jason, was bringing it all up again. Through him, that fear of someone wanting to "get me" was coming back. I started wetting my bed, which I hadn't done since I was two years old.

Flashing back, it brought up my situation in France too, when that dark-robed figure appeared in my room, again terrifying me. Obviously it was time to release this fear, hopefully to get beyond it.

We started having disagreements and then misunderstandings about my land. He was beginning to feel that half of it should belong to him, and that I owed him half. We were not married and ours was a very basic no-cost living situation. He had nothing to pay as it was free rent for us both. And I appreciated his skill at making our living situation easier.

But undoubtedly Jason felt that he was progressing toward something of value, upgrading our living situation, which he felt should be accounted for. I'd paid for the cheap land and the fencing around the forty acres; it was all I had.

However, I knew the issue brought up a family situation whereby he had an agreement with his father and his business in Reno, Nevada. Jason co-worked with him for a designated number of years at a lower salary, under the agreement that the business would be his after those years were done. But when that time was up, his father declared he wasn't ready and refused to hand it over. Jason, devastated, left. His marriage broke up at the same time.

Unfortunately he harbored a very strong anger that still lingered deep inside him. In any moment, reacting to a situation that didn't involve me, he could engage this deep anger and direct it at me. A few times I was scared and feared for my safety.

I tried to avoid speaking about the land, but he brought it up often, wanting to have an answer. I gave him no definitive reply, but he seemed to get more anxious. I had no intention of giving him half the land, being unsure of our future together now, so it seemed unfair to say "yes." Thus I gave him no answer.

One morning when I was sitting on the couch area of the main trailer reading the paper, he came in showing fire in his eyes, his lips tightly pressed together.

"Are you going to give me half of this property?" he asked, standing directly in front of me.

"Don't know yet, I'll have to see, something," I answered timidly before he thrust out his right hand, bent over and swung it toward my face. Protecting myself, I turned my shoulder to him as his hand hit hard, stinging my upper arm. I cried out, *"Ouch"*, grasping my arm and shoulder. "There," he said and stepped out of the trailer. I stayed waiting to see what he might do next, still rubbing my arm from the sting.

As the situation escalated, I was desperate, and began planning how and when I could get off the land, back to Sedona, without much money. I went into my valuable family belongings stored in the other trailer.

As soon as Jason left to get water, I walked around to the storage trailer entrance. Opening it, I went in to find my boxes from back east. Reaching over my boxes of 35mm book negatives, boxes full of my exhibition prints, I finally located the boxes with the family silver.

I opened a few delicately with a sharp knife. Yes, my favorite set of silverware was there, but I looked deeper in the box for the Hallmark collector's items, several silver spoons and a pie cutter, which I took out to sell. Then I opened the tightly sealed box of antique plates and chose a few English dark blue and white ones.

I selected some beautiful old Irish linens and the simple, brass telescope of my father's I always admired. Carefully camouflaging them, the next day I drove south to the bigger city of Show Low to an antique store. Fortunately they loved my antiques and bought every single item from me. Putting the money in the bank that had a branch in Sedona, I waited for the right moment.

Driving back to my barren land, while opening the gate, I asked myself:

How much longer was I willing to let myself be stuck out here in someone else's dream, forsaking my own? Where did MY dream go? In fact, what was it anyway?

One evening soon after, walking alone with the dogs in the glorious pinks of the setting sun, a voice came into my head wanting to be heard. It was calling me to something, but then it got louder for me to hear it clearly: *Where are you? I am waiting....*

Oops.... I knew it was Magdalene calling me back to France. She was trying to remind me of something I had stepped away from. It had actually been a few years since I'd been back to France. *Wow, that long?* I said to myself.

A day later at a flea market, I brought one of my expensive family end tables, one that I could not imagine using anytime soon, and sold it for one tenth of its value. Jason was selling crystals from his large collection while friends, a couple, were next to us selling T- shirts with designs they'd printed on them.

As it began to get late in the day, we all decided to pack up what was left. Gathering my last few items, a short round stool, I stepped over to put it inside my car. I lifted the door of my Honda wagon, which swung upward. Normally it stayed there until I was ready to close it.

But suddenly out of nowhere, the hatchback door swung down as if someone were pushing it hard from the other side, with the strength of a 40 mile an hour wind. *Klunk!* It landed hard on the bridge of my nose.

Crying out in pain, I bent over, certain my nose was broken. The man from the couple sprinted over and quickly placed his hand over my nose, holding it there for more than half an hour, when the pain finally subsided. Assessing it after, no, it wasn't broken, but it ended up leaving a visible scar.

OK, I said to myself, *This is my wakeup call! This is the final blow!* Two days later I got up early and packed my car. My year and a half experience on my land was over.

I waited for Jason to get up and come out of his trailer, as we were sleeping in different places. He was shaken by my decision, probably not surprised, as our relationship was already strained. I had to get away right then. I was being called back to Sedona, to France, now!

We said our goodbyes, but said I would be back to visit and get my stuff. I drove down the dirt driveway to the gate, stopped, opened it and looked back down the winding road at Jason standing there surrounded by the three dogs. Then I turned back and got into my car, drove through the gate and closed it behind me. My land experience was over.

While driving the highway toward Snowflake, emotions overcame me as tears fell so heavily they blurred the road before me. I pulled over.

Leaving Jason had not caused this emotion; it was my whole life that I had put on hold, my lost dreams. I asked myself, why had I done this? Two months, or six months was OK for an adventure, but to be out there, in a situation like this for almost two years?

I had nothing now as I sank deep, looking into what was before me, assuring myself, *I will find myself again*. I soon learned that even my Sedona friends had written me off, unsure if I would ever return from my land situation.

Yes, I went to the depths of *letting go* of most everything, which later I compared to the ancient legend of the Babylonian Goddess *Ianna*. She also made a life-changing journey.

Thousands of years ago she descended into the underworld through seven gateways. At each gate she let go of something that had protected her and gave her strength, to figuratively die when she arrived at the bottom.

Once there she had to identify her deepest pain, meet herself at the darkest level of her own shadow. By experiencing what was there she could gain a new understanding. Moreover, her journey was to see it, accept it and then turn the pain around, by retrieving what she had left behind. Thus as she ascended into the upper world, she knew who she was.

Similarly my journey was now about coming back up. Hopefully I would be carrying a deeper knowing of who I was at the core. By seeing, feeling and re-experiencing my greatest fears, they dissolved. They seemed to be gone.

I could feel that the "fluff" was gone from my life; I was going to be more direct with the world. What that meant however, I had no idea. To start, I had no real attachments.

Chapter 25 - In The Flames Of The Fire

A ray of light came down from the heavens and shined on me. I looked up to see its source. I was sprawled out on the floor next to six other women with our heads angled toward the center. Suzanne, my new employer at "Sedona Vortex Tours and Retreats" was amongst us as one of our company members demonstrated a meditation she offered clients.

We were lying down in a room next to the main office. It had been infused with energies of light and love, so we would weave it into our meditative state, surrendering effortlessly, after each had set an intention.

As I closed my eyes, my inner experience took me to a place I had not seen before, where I had an immediate communication. My intention had been to: *Find the next level of my work in the world.*

While the beam directed itself at me, I looked up and saw a *Being* wearing a white robe who said he was from the *high council.* Appearing to be with others, he was the one watching me, who, with no hesitation, told me that they were indeed calling me to the next level of my "work."

Bathing myself in this ray of white light, I wanted to remember this moment, this *Being*, anxious to know where it would lead me. It seemed something magical was calling me.

My return to Sedona was smooth. I stayed with a friend until I found work, as a spiritual guide, a vortex guide and also offered medicine wheel ceremonies out on Sedona's red rocks. I realized that my experience of living so close to the land for nearly two years gave me courage, a new strength that also allowed me to be one of the few guides taking people out on vision quests overnight. I had no fears. I also had gained a deeper sense of compassion for others.

Then a new friend also working at Vortex Tours asked if I wanted to share an apartment. I said *"Yes,"* reflecting on my primitive living experiences on the land. An apartment felt like an invitation back to a new life, beckoning me to step back into the normal world. Interestingly, we moved in on May 1st, the powerful Beltane cross quarter day that had played a significant part in much of my Priestess work, certainly in France.

Most of my belongings were still out on the land, however, so I would have to go out and retrieve them. They were stored in the trailer Jason and I had cleaned out.

As we finished moving into our new apartment, it had been a long day, when suddenly, after sitting to rest for a moment, a loud ring cut through my meditation. It was the phone so I got up to answer it.

I listened to the voice at the other end. My heart sank, "NO...NO," I said, dropping to the ground in shock. I slipped into a void that felt like an eternity from which I never wanted to come out. It was Jason telling me that the generator had miss-fired and blown up. It burned everything in the storage trailer.

Days before my departure I noticed it on the porch near the entrance of the trailer and didn't have a good feeling about it, although it had just been repaired.

"We lost everything! Everything in the trailer is gone," he said. "But everything else on the property was saved. Not one tree was burned and the animals are safe."

All my negatives were there, from my books and perspective books and 11 years of photographs from sacred sites. There were several large four foot black and white prints from past photo shows, boxes of exhibition prints and all my holography equipment – lasers, optics, magnetic bases, including the steel topped table Los Alamos had built for the holography program I did in 1992.

Ancestral family items were stored there, furniture, antique plates and lots of silver, all sizes, after my brother, sisters and I had sold our family home on Martha's Vineyard. All my personal things including photos from my wedding, Priestess ordinations and sacred ceremonial objects were there.

Seriously looking at the size of my new apartment, I had questioned before where I would store all these things tagging along from my past. The next day I drove over to see what was there, if there was anything remaining and I wanted to support Jason in the devastating tragedy he had just witnessed. He too lost everything.

Curiously, Beltane, May 1st was also when fires were traditionally lit along hilltops all across Britain, in fact all over Europe. The timing was most interesting, it being the same day I moved into my new apartment.

The gate was open. I drove in heading for the trailer or now the log building. I noticed the dark colored sand behind it and the burned rubble still smelling as I opened my window. The invisible flames still lingered in the energy. Luckily it was the neighbors who called the fire department when they noticed the flames.

I had no feelings yet, unsure of my reaction. For a photographer, back in the days when we still worked with negatives, a fire was your worst nightmare. If the negatives are gone, all was lost. Worse, I had all my expensive exhibition prints and holography equipment there too. Curiously I had let go of my photography career little by little and after meeting Jason, I put it aside for my singular spiritual path.

I parked and stepped out of the car, greeted by the dogs and Jason. He was still devastated, lost in shock. I noticed his face the palest I'd ever seen it, his eyes had lost their shine, his cheeks almost sunken and his heart energy felt constricted as if nothing were left inside. He was devoid of any warmth. *Was he going to hold himself responsible for the seeming disaster,* I wondered.

I couldn't reassure him because I wasn't sure of my own feelings after such a great loss. The mounds of sand on the land had probably helped ground the fire so it wasn't able to spread. In fact a lot appeared hidden amongst the rubble and in the sand, ashes.

Slowly I walked over to the back area where my things were in the trailer to see what was there. I saw a few things sticking out of the sand. I went over to touch a burned piece of silver, pulling it out, all blackened. Then I saw a few other pieces of half hidden silver, knowing I would have to spend more time searching, but this wasn't the moment.

I moved over, kneeling on the blackened ashes and dug deeper. I found a burned print. Continuing, I found a second one, then a third. They had been layered together in a box. I pulled them out, realizing there were probably others and that I would have to wash them to identify what image might be remaining, but another time.

As I stood surrounded by this debris, the remains of what my life had been identifying who I was in my earlier life, words blurted out of my mouth, "Thank You."

From a deep place within, I acknowledged that I had asked for this, after the intention I'd made in my friend's meditation a week earlier. The *high council* member heard my words and sent a beam of light down to me, affirming they would help me find the next level of my *work in the world.* Curiously, I felt no attachments to what I had lost and there was no emotion. I was grateful.

Chapter 26 – Where Would She Speak To Me?

Magdalene called me a second time, thinking I didn't hear her first call, while still deep in my land experience. But I did.

How could I forget that cold, silent, midnight eve, shivering in front of the Tour Magdala when she appeared to me with her long sword, asking if I would *Do Her Story*. I'd replied *Yes,* but hadn't written it yet. In fact, I wanted to know *what that story was she wanted me to tell.* She was still waiting.

I knew she would find me somewhere in France, but where that was I didn't know. My next journey back to France might lead me to places I'd never been, where Mary Magdalene was known to have possibly taught, passed briefly or died. Furthermore, the journey would require attuning very carefully to my *inner voice to find where she wanted to speak to me.*

Gathering the necessary money, Paris was my first stop. I was inspired to begin by visiting places from my previous life in France when my identity was as a photographer, a photojournalist. Maybe after loosing all my negatives, including those from my French Peasant story, there was a desire inside to reclaim something even if it was only a memory.

Many times I traveled to Paris to make prints from the black and white film I'd developed on the farm where I was staying. It always felt disorienting for me to step from a timeless lifetime, long ago, when people were still walking behind oxen, plowing or harvesting their crops manually, into the Paris experience of fast cars, trains and bright city lights.

Acclimating, I stayed with one of my two friends, both respected picture editors for Paris magazines who were familiar with my photo project. Surprisingly a French magazine did a story on me at that time and then I was honored to have a photographic exhibition there of my peasant photographs.

But now my life had changed. One friend had reservations after my attempts to explain my new focus of working with the feminine, Magdalene. Our worlds were different now.

During my few days in Paris, I made a visit to the left bank and the famous Notre Dame Cathedral. After crossing the bridge over the famous *Seine River,* I walked under the multilayered gothic doorway of the Cathedral. Moving down the central isle under the high gothic ceilings I sat at the place of "crossing" where the horizontal arms crossed the vertical length of the church.

As I faced the main altar area, a warm sensation surrounded me, seeming to carry a golden light. After I relaxed into it, suddenly, something forced me to get up and run outside. A disturbance moved in, something that felt dense, dark.

Once outside, I found an isolated black iron bench opposite the cathedral and quickly sat down. A very charged message wanted to express itself to me, saying:

They have tried to put a box around who I Am, to keep it contained, but I Am endless, timeless, untouchable in their ways. Their symbols do not do justice to the energies and magnitude of my being, to the essence of what I Am. I Am all that is, was or ever has been and I say come to me and surrender. I am calling you. Listen to your heart.

I listened to these words carefully hoping her message could help me understand what she was reacting to, what had happened there. Of course I was aware of the bigger picture of the suppressed, lost feminine spirit. But more specifically I knew that there was a black Madonna hidden below in this church, away from the gaze of the crowds who came to see the cathedral. In fact, the name Paris comes from the name *Isis, Par-Isis* as there was once an ancient temple to her nearby, if not right here,.

After visiting a few more places, I took the train down to southwestern France and finally arrived at my favorite B&B, Les Angelos, in Rennes Les Bains. Rose, now a close friend, greeted me warmly. Les Angelos felt like home for me, situated above the familiar Sals River.

That first day, I knew it was important for me to do a shamanic journey and make a connection with that dark-robed being who had caused my arrest here the last time. I wanted to inform him of my intention to not disturb them again that they had their work to do, as did I, mine. From this moment, everything I did on the land was low key, subtle and I never encountered them again.

Focusing now on Magdalene and where she might speak to me, I made several visits to Rennes Le Chateau. I went over to sit in front of the Tour Magdala, resting my back against the foundation near where I originally buried the *despacho*, that chilly midnight on May 1, 1998.

I called out, *Oh great Magdalene, Isis and guardians of this ancient site, please join me now from your distant realms. Forgive this long wait, but now I have returned and am waiting to hear your words once again.*

Hoping the tall being would again appear before me with her sword, I came back several times, and waited and waited, patiently, but no one came. Reluctantly, I accepted that there was somewhere else she was calling me to find her.

With a knowing, I set off on a solo journey to Les Saints Maries de la Mers for counsel with St. Sarah, the dark Madonna known either as the patron saint of the gypsies or the daughter of Mary Magdalene and Jesus. Having only been there once, I got clear directions for the five-hour drive. A small fishing town, it was located in a district called the Camargue, known as the cowboy country of France I learned. When the land flattened out, I saw lagoons alive with pink flamingos just before my arrival in the quaint Mediterranean village.

A famous beach town, it was not far from Marseilles and where Mary Magdalene was known to have arrived from the Holy Land two thousand years ago. Legends say she was with her sister Martha, two other Marys, Sarah, her brother Lazarus and possibly Joseph of Arimethea. In fact the gypsies still celebrate the famous arrival each year with a festival at the end of May.

I learned that the ancient church was fortified in the 6th century and housed the statue of St. Sarah in its crypt, where hundreds of people came each year to say prayers and light candles near her statue.

After entering the side door of the church, I walked down the aisle, and ducked my head as I stepped down the stairs into the crypt. It was hot from the many burning candles, as I moved over in front of St. Sarah, face to face. She was covered with soft satiny robes, layers of them, white, pink, light blue, all wrapped around her by gypsies during the last ceremonial events.

Her dark eyes looked directly at me, their whites seemingly brighter in this low-lit room. I grasped one of her robes, a light blue one between two fingers and asked her to help me reclaim my life.

Then I asked that she heal any sexual wounds or shame that had come up during my past relationships. Immediately I heard her tell me, *Go and purify yourself in the salt waters of the Mediterranean*, after which I gave thanks and stepped back so the next person standing nearby could have a turn.

Looking around for a hotel, I found one down a quiet street, *The Neptune* where I would spend several days, walking the beaches, relaxing and asking for healing and guidance from St. Sarah.

When, on my second night, a whisk of cool energy woke me in the middle of the night, I opened my eyes to discern the vision of a dark face, saying, *You are on the right path, follow where you are being called*. I knew it was St. Sarah. She was answering my call, supporting me on my mission after I had asked for her help.

The next day, sitting by the soothing waters of a nearby pond, a lagoon, I watched the pink flamingos take off and land. It was so peaceful that I silently slipped off into an experience that many refer to as a *samadi* state in which I felt so blissful, my question was if I could ever move to go anywhere else.

Only a day later I received the message to depart for the Basilica of Mary Magdalene in St. Maximin, so I organized myself carefully and looked closely at the map. Maybe an hour and a half drive, I, in my state of bliss, have no recollection of how I got there.

After finding the motor route east marked with signs to St. Maximin, I turned off to the small village. I liked its simplicity and parked my car near the village square. Outdoor restaurants were on the corners, with streets leading to the Basilica, so I chose one and followed it.

The Basilica's façade went straight up, almost a sheer sheet of light sand-colored stone, where a gold and red striped flag hung over the doorway. I entered, marveling at the immensity of the church with its high gothic arches, numerous paintings and sculptures worth studying carefully. After walking down the main isle toward the wooden benches in front of the altar area, I sat down.

Here, in this Basilica, I learned that the skull of Mary Magdalene is kept in the crypt, and which, supposedly, had been "lost" for over a thousand years, they said. After centuries of wars during which many relics disappeared or were destroyed, evidently it was safe again to display her skull.

Down steps that turned twice, below the left central area of the Basilica, I found the entrance to the crypt and went down. I passed a sculpture of Magdalene lying on her side in a low lit area along the way. Then, at the bottom suspended on a platform was her *skull.* It was behind a casing. I moved over to experience the energies emanating from it that might offer me something of value. Standing with my heart open, a faint feeling of warmth touched me, but it was not strong.

On both sides of the small compact room were panels of carvings on a dark slab of stone; to one side they depicted Biblical stories of something that was once important, while on the other to my left, the one that caught my attention had whales, small fish and then a dark figure, half man-half fish. I realized it might be associated with the *Merovingians*, the first lineage of French kings that were said to come from the water and connected to Jesus' lineage. But that was another story.

I climbed back up the stairs and left the Basilica, having no sense at all that the skull belonged to Mary Magdalene. Interestingly, they celebrated Magdalene's Feast Day, July 22 here, each year. Crowds arrive to follow the procession through the streets behind the skull encased in gold for the occasion. Evidently, they have done this for hundreds of years to honor Mary Magdalene.

Complete, I was told to continue to explore the cave where many legends declared that Magdalene had died, after 30 years of communing with the angels. This was a route I might not have found easily had I not asked for specific directions from a young man at the café there.

Climbing over the high mountain pass in my small French car, I found the Dominican *Hostellerie*. It was located below the high white cliffs where this famous cave, the *Grotte de St. Baume* was located. The cliffs reminded me of the Hopi Mesas of northeastern Arizona, where they built their villages thousands of years ago.

Luckily, when learning of this place, I had called to reserve a room for several nights hosted by the Dominican Sisters. Not Catholic, I was invited to stay there with respectful reverence.

When I stepped into the small office I met one of the sisters dressed in her blue nun's outfit. She checked me in and gave me the times and details for breakfast and simple dinner if I wanted it.

My room on the second floor was one of the many doorways along the barren hallway, the last room on the left. A communal shower and bathroom were opposite. My room had one single bed, a small table and a lamp; I liked the simplicity, but more important I liked the view from the window of the distant cliffs with a tiny building on top.

Remote, the Hostellerie was hundreds of years old, I learned. A simple, clean monastic place of lodging, it was mostly for Catholics on retreat. Evidently it had once hosted the French kings coming to pay homage to Magdalene.

Then I walked down the stairs to explore the famous chapel close by the office. It displayed beautiful murals on the walls, with one of Magdalene standing outside her high cave from which legend says she ascended. Another shows her standing on the shore along the Mediterranean coast holding up a cross. Several boats were in front of her carrying people I assumed were there to hear her teachings.

After exploring the grounds, I went to bed. Breakfast was early and I wanted to take what looked like a strenuous hike up to the cave after. Sitting next to an enthusiastic middle-aged woman and her husband at breakfast, both religious, they quickly offered to show me the best path up to the cave. She mentioned that it was one of the days the Brothers offered a service. I also learned that they served as guardians up there and lived in the small hermitage next to it.

The path traversed upward, shaded by forest trees on each side. Tiny pieces of gravel moved noisily under my feet before the path then transformed into packed soil. Hidden groves on one side or the other showed where people might once have stopped to rest or camp long ago.

The magic of this forest felt like it was leading me into worlds of fairies and elves who seemed to be watching from their rock hideaways or twisted tree stumps, waiting for a moment to tell their stories.

I was quickly informed that this was the most famous forest in all of France, covered with trees not found anywhere else. Thus people came to identify and marvel at the many species alongside this ascending path.

Back and forth we moved. People of all ages, backgrounds and countries, walked this path together. I climbed the path next to other men and women, some short, some tall, some with twisted bodies laboring with determination to reach the top. And some moved easily over the terrain.

Sometimes long branches extended over the path, as if they were the arms of the great forest mother encouraging everyone to arrive safely at the top, supporting them from behind.

We were walking the Path of the Kings, *Le Chemin des Rois*, on which, I learned from the lady walking next to me, these kings were known to have walked up on their knees. Evidently it was to show reverence to the Magdalene and the sacredness of this cave, whether she died here or not.

While climbing the last stairs to reach the grotto, I spotted a terrace outside where people could rest and gaze at the breathtaking view below. They could marvel at the path on which they had come. Quickly I saw that the original wide cave opening had been enclosed and made into a small door we opened to enter.

I entered, forgetting that caves could be so cold, where I found a large group gathered on benches below the high rock altar, anticipating the sermon. Inside the rock enclosure, I walked around to see what I could before the Dominican Brother began his sermon. Behind the altar I noticed a small glass container with one relic bone, carefully displayed, supposedly belonging to Magdalene. Then on the back wall I found a nice sculpted statue of Magdalene, surrounded by angels.

Too soon however the priest began his sermon, so I returned and found a place in the back. I listened, but was not comfortable so I got up to quietly slip out the door, hoping my departure went unnoticed.

Interestingly, two days before leaving Sedona, I met an Australian woman who was familiar with this St. Baume area and encouraged me to search for another cave, another place where Magdalene might have been.

Keeping her words in mind, I found another path, one I had seen marked on my way up. It led to the tiny chapel at the highest point of this mountain ridge, the same one I'd seen from my room window. But it was much steeper climb, so I had to carefully navigate over the rocks, softened by centuries of eager footsteps that wore down their original craggy surfaces.

At the top another path traversed the high cliff area over to the tiny chapel, the *Chapel de Pilot.* I proceeded carefully, anxious to reach this tiny isolated chapel.

Arriving outside, I took a breath as I peered in through the vertical bars at a statue of Mary Magdalene. She was standing carrying a special jar in her arms, the alabaster jar I assumed. A circular opening appeared in the ceiling.

The energy was so strong; I searched in my backpack to find one of the tiny candles I'd brought. I bent down and lit it, placing it on a ledge as I said a prayer. The Magdalene figure was behind bars probably for her protection, but it was also very symbolic of the bigger picture of her story, I thought.

Exhilarated, I loved the energy of this high place and soon began to explore, in search of something it felt I was meant to discover. With several choices of places to go, I noticed an oblong elevated rock ridge area below, and off to my right. I thought it might possibly be harboring a hidden cave opening so I pursued it.

Enthusiastically, I circled this elevated rock ridge hoping to find the place where Magdalene would speak to me. I spent hours walking completely around it looking into every niche or dark place that might have an opening to a cave. But there were no entrances or mystical openings.

It became three long hours of searching under the hot sun. Then finally I settled down to rest. Choosing to be near the small Magdalene chapel, I decided to let go and stop trying so hard to find anything. I was tired. It was time to surrender, with no concerns about what was next.

I closed my eyes and laid back on the white rocks, knowing when I opened them it would be time to descend back down the steep path and find my way to the Hostellerie.

When, reluctantly, I opened my eyes, my gaze fixed on a small bush coming out of a crevice in front of me. Curious, I got up and walked over to see from where it was growing. Bees were humming all around the bush. It seemed to be camouflaging an opening to somewhere, so I stretched my neck out to look inside. I saw a steep tunnel going straight down into darkness, *It must be going to somewhere*, I said to myself, wondering.

Instinctively, I left my backpack outside the opening and courageously stepped down into it. Yes, bees were everywhere; I let them swarm around me as I extended my legs down to touch the only flat rock on the inside ledge. Here I sat.

Sitting above this drop-off place, bees moved all around my body, my face, my hands, my back and legs, but I wasn't afraid. And then I heard a voice speak to me:

You have arrived. It has been a long journey since we last met and now you are here. Welcome. Many have assisted you along the way, but this is where you were called to be. This has been a pilgrimage for you and now we shall begin.

It is time to reveal the story that has long been hidden within you. When you walk the path of the Feminine, it is not only my story, it is also your story and you are here to tell it now. It is time to remember, I am with you so do not forget this.

I thought she was done speaking but she continued:

It is time for you to write, do small pieces and publish them, get started. Your life will begin to change as you watch how you are re-directed, making new decisions and plans for what you want to offer in the world. You will begin to remember 'who you are' and what you are here to do.

Yes, I said to myself after, *She has found me!* And I listened to every word, every suggestion she gave me, totally surrendered, present. Her words were what I had come to hear, all the way to France. But it was bigger than that; it was about the *truth* of a pilgrimage, the *journey*, beyond my adventures, beyond my diversions. Letting go of everything was the only way I could have made a deeper commitment to myself.

Uplifted, I climbed out of my small niche hole and gratefully turned to thank the bees. Then I sat on top for a minute and honored myself, before walking over to the Magdalene Chapel. My candle was still burning so I gave thanks to Magdalene for calling me here.

I followed the trail along the ridge to where it would meet the steep path below. I climbed down the overhanging cliff carefully ready to navigate my way back down to the Hostellerie. My mission had been accomplished in France for now. *She had spoken to me.*

Complete, the next day I drove back to Rennes Les Bains, then to Toulouse; I flew back to Phoenix and then arrived, finally, in Sedona. I did everything Magdalene suggested and my life changed; it literally turned around. I felt my earlier intention of following the path of the feminine return. Only now I was walking with a deeper wisdom not only about myself but about life in general. I was beginning to remember who I was, my calling, not only in this lifetime, but from long ago.

Chapter 27 - Moving to France

O nce in the air, I closed my eyes and leaned back in my seat. I took a few deep breaths in and let them out, releasing all the stress from packing.

During my last release, as I was settling in for a deserved twelve hour rest on the plane with dinner, there they were...*the council...in their white robes.* They were above me, shining the same light ray down as before in the meditation at Vortex Tours. They were with me.

It was 2006 and I would be arriving on my birthday, March 2nd, ready to occupy my new apartment in Rennes Les Bains. Destiny had made the decision for me late October of 2005; my second group that year left to fly back to the US.

Staying on, I remember walking the path by the Sals River and sitting on a weathered wooden bench. I glanced across the river at a row of houses when my right index finger suddenly raised itself up and pointed to the house with the big willow tree in the back yard, declaring to myself, *This is where I want to live, in that house!*

The next day while having lunch with a new friend from Rennes Le Chateau, she looked up while swallowing a spoonful of potato leek soup and asked me, "Are you looking for an apartment?" Taken aback, I hesitated before giving my answer, "I'm not sure, well....Yes...maybe. Why?" She replied, "Because my friend has a wonderful house in Rennes Les Bains and is trying to rent one of the apartments in it."

"Great," I said, "Yes, I'm interested." She mentioned it had a lovely willow tree in the backyard, so of course I knew which house it was. It was two or three houses away from the church in Rennes Les Bains and the other side of the small village from Rose's B&B, Les Angelos.

Finally arriving, I lifted the latch of the low iron gate set back from the sidewalk and went down the concrete stairs to the bottom. I went around the corner of this three-story house, and found the stairs up to my new apartment.

From here I could see the entire backyard that stretched to the River Sals, with the tall willow tree near the end. Other trees and bushes helped mark the property's boundaries. Inside, the main room had a dining table and a two-burner stove. The cupboard with all the dishes rested along the opposite wall and a nice blue couch was placed at the center of the room.

The bedroom had a tall wooden hutch and a short dresser for clothes. By the window facing the back yard was a padded olive green chair with a high back, perfect, I thought, to sit and meditate in the morning or evenings. When I passed through a smaller bedroom next to the bathroom, I was excited to see a bathtub. They are not common in French apartments.

It had all the furniture I needed, for now, though a few weeks later, a friend drove me to a place where I bought a small desk and several chairs for the second bedroom, which I made into my office. I also found a square rug to put in front of the couch, as the French do not value carpeting or rugs like Americans do.

I loved the back yard and I sat under the weeping willow tree often, especially as it got warmer. I liked to go down and sit close by the Sals River or swish my feet in the water to nurture myself on a more daily basis, after living in the high desert for so long. Here I could walk to my favorite places along the river, replenishing my energies any time of day.

But before leaving Sedona, I wrote several short articles for a local magazine, continued leading tours for the company I worked for and sold my land. In fact, a week after the fire on my land, the largest fire in all of Arizona started burning thirty miles from the property.

Jason's father bought him a large RV, so he too left the land. The property sold, but nothing we had built on it had any monetary value; evidently the foundation Jason had built didn't follow the proper codes. Thus the property value was the same, the fence cost added.

I had led two trips to France in 2005 focused on Mary Magdalene and the Feminine, inviting participants to explore the mysteries of not only the Rennes Le Chateau and Rennes Les Bains areas, but other places where Magdalene had walked. I made sure to take each group to St. Baume and that remote cave opening high on the cliffs next to the Magdalene Chapel. I wanted to pass the place of my life-changing experience on to others.

My apartment became a wonderful sanctuary for me. After moving my clothes, books and other items to France, I would stay as long as I needed. In fact I had three groups coming in 2006. Two were back-to-back that fall with Priestesses from the east coast, Georgia and Kansas, whom I had never met. Everyone had gone through Nicole's *Priestess Awakening Process* and some had been facilitating their own groups for years now.

Unusual wisdom continued to be given to me in France during my trips or in between them, intended for the bigger story of the Feminine. It was not only giving details about the ancient Temple Mysteries deep in the earth beneath Rennes Les Bains, but the ancient Priestesses and their timeless work on the planet.

Often it felt as if I were living in two worlds, seeing deeper into places that were still holding mysteries, where more authentic realities were still playing out. Several times I wasn't sure if I would step back into this physical reality, but luckily my shamanic background after so many years helped give me a strong foundation to be present in the 3-D world.

For instance each time I visited the *Fountain des Amors* (the Fountain of Loves), one of my favorite places, I had a mystical experience. Crossing the bridge after Rennes Les Bains where the two rivers meet, La Blanque and La Sals, I would drive the windy road a short distance and leave my car on the side.

The path down to the creek escorted me through a line of tall trees that serve to sanctify the sacredness of this place. At the end of it, a small spring drips almost unnoticed in the "place of the Goddess," who I always stopped to honor before continuing to reach the fountain's larger pool.

Salt waters flowing from the La Source Sale above, passed through here. They flow by the smaller heart-shaped pond, near ruins of an ancient hermitage left centuries ago. This magical place was one where I liked to be.

Sometimes I crossed over to the tiny heart-shaped pond to sit where a salamander had been carved on the rock under the hermitage ruins.

Later a new friend told me that La Fountain des Amors is known to be a place where beings gather from all worlds, to meet and share love.

For instance I was told that people might come to renew a vow of love, or bring a new love hoping to receive information about whether it would work out or not. Or they come to have an encounter of love, not knowing from which world it might arrive.

One time in late November when no one else was there, I walked down between the line of trees, feeling the ground's softness under my boots. It was still moist from two days of solid rain. The water was flowing fast and high through this ancient place, on its way to meet the river below, so I sat down across from and facing the smaller heart pond.

"Oh my God, " I suddenly exclaimed, "It's another diamond experience," when, sure enough, a diamond suspended itself before me. *What was going to happen this time*, I questioned, curious.

It was a very, very large diamond-shaped vehicle with Beings inside it. Watching more closely I saw how each was able to select a small portion in which they could place themselves, which then broke off to become its own individual diamond, a miniature. Immediately I remembered the being appearing outside my balcony window in Sedona, in its own diamond vehicle.

Amazed, I was being shown that by making themselves small enough to fit inside a miniature diamond-shaped vehicle, they could travel easily by themselves. Then I received more information of why they did this, explaining:

It was so they could 'seed' chosen places with specific 'codes' and be undetected. It began with beings coming to earth from one star constellation, one system and then other beings learned of the possibilities here, so they followed suit.

However a code was necessary to enable the coming and going of these tiny diamonds. Guardians were at the doorways watching, knowing when to open them. Each location carried a special code of how it related to the planetary system above or sometimes to the waters below, which might have a 'sun' or a special 'object' hidden there. This object would help align and turn the wheels or axis angles of the Earth. La Fountain des Amors is one such place.

I learned that the depths of the waters here are unknown, even after Jacques Costeau, the famous French diver, made a dive here hoping to find the bottom, but found none.

Fascinated, I then received another piece of information about what might be happening here:

Mermaid people can grow here in their pods. They are planted within the waters here to adjust and familiarize themselves with the energy. They then take 'readings' on the vibrations beneath the water so they know where, when and what exactly to do.

Mermaids were highly trained to know these things and came from ancient lineages and places vibrating on the highest level. They were either trained for years or for millennia, before coming to a place like Earth where they would fine-tune the systems being set up here.

Each had a special shape or symbol she worked with. Then together in the pods, something powerful happened, as they helped create alignments for the sake of the planets, universes, so all could be connected.

Often I brought groups here to facilitate an inner marriage ceremony, inviting each person to connect with his or her beloved within, seeing what was misaligned, if anything, so they could correct it.

A special memory I have is of the small circle of women I worked with for the two years when I lived here. It was late October when we had just finished doing an inner marriage ceremony here.

Without any hesitation, the women quickly de-robed and immersed themselves - as a mermaid would -

in this sacred pond into these very, very cold waters. For a short time I imagined the women were these timeless beings, mermaids, seemingly unaffected by the temperature, peeking their heads out of the pond as a mermaid might.

But then suddenly they all began shrieking, realizing that the water temperature was much too cold for their bodies to endure for long. As fast as possible they all climbed out of the water grasping for warm clothes.

Unmistakably, this was a portal place between the worlds.

Chapter 28 - My Lost Soul Piece

L ate one afternoon, months after my move to France, I was sitting on my blue couch meditating, when I heard: *You are here to heal your heart, from past lifetimes*.

It was the *Beings in the white robes*, *"the council"*, speaking, who said, *We want to work with you, make it easy for you. If you will follow us now through this dark tunnel we have something to show you*.

Oops, I quickly flashed on several times during my earlier France visits, when I was also aware of beings wanting to lead me down some dark tunnel to show me something. But I wouldn't go. Each time I said, *No!* Curiously, after all my years of doing shamanic journeys into dark tunnels to get somewhere else, I still wouldn't go.

But this time, I was ready. I lay back on the blue couch and closed my eyes. I knew who they were, that they were looking out for me, helping me with something that might change my life. So I followed them.

They guided me through a tunnel down, down, moving in one direction then another when finally I arrived somewhere dim, where I saw an object. It was an odd shape with circular symbols and patterns marked all over it.

Then I saw and felt images of myself, as if I were looking down an eerie corridor at some of my past lives in France. I saw myself as a Priestess and then saw other scenes. I loved a Templar or someone I was not supposed to love. I saw beautiful blue patterns…and then something happened. I was lost in darkness.

Help, blurted out from deep inside my psyche. I was very scared. It was a very dark place. Maybe I had been buried there…..or had been killed there. Then my exploratory journey ended and I sat up.

Shocked and choked up, I had just seen myself buried deep in the Earth. I called out to Mary Magdalene to please come and help me so I could learn the truth about what I was seeing. Soon she arrived and delivered this message:

It is not in the darkness where you have been placed, but in other dimensions, at the portal, as the time keeper of when to release this highly guarded information. You have been trying to secure that you will never be lost again, with no way back. If you can trust us to guide you, this information coming forth, through you, will be in the right time. Do Not Fear. There Is Only Love. Your time has come.

Slightly relieved, I thanked her, hoping she was right.

Later that day I went outside to focus on this object I'd seen deep in the Earth and was told to get ready to download something into my chest, my heart. Under the long wispy branches of the willow tree, lying on my lounge chair, I called my lost heart piece back to me.

I began to cry a lot, feeling my vulnerability and complete surrender. Enhancing this situation was the fact that I started a relationship with a younger French man who I met here six months previous. However, after moving here I thought that I was meant to stay alone in my apartment, being called on some kind of "mission". He started seeing someone else, which hurt me deeply. It brought up my vulnerable heart.

Again I was addressing my heart issues, old relationships and my part in each, looking at being loved and loving and the many levels of love and choices I had made. Thinking I had already addressed this issue in my Magdalene process, I guessed not. This was a deeper level. I questioned how open or closed I was to receiving, to giving, exploring the depths of my heart issues.

My sadness took me to such depths that I sobbed and sobbed and then fell asleep, sobbing. When I woke up, I was still in the same fetal position, the same chair, having not moved. It had been almost three hours. All the pain lodged within my heart for so many lifetimes was coming out.

Again I called my heart back, when four more lifetimes came up from this region, a Knights Templar, a Cathar and Priestess ones, an older woman with a younger man, afraid to lose my heart, then a lost love situation and then a fear of losing something I loved dearly… as it continued.

I realized this was a big 'issue' in my present lifetime that perhaps had also come from many past experiences here: guarding my heart, not to love too deeply, too passionately. I was afraid of love or…. life. It seemed like I was always holding myself back.

After recognizing this, my heart got warmer, the way it does when I do *soul retrievals* for others and know when their lost soul essence is returning to them. While this was happening, something seeming *otherworldly* was becoming visible. I recognized the Little Cascade and then saw what appeared to be a large ship, like a UFO, anchoring something into the area, maybe energy. Realizing that perhaps I had been taken up on this ship, I saw pearl-like lights inside surrounding a seat in the center.

Observing what exactly was happening the way I do while performing soul retrievals for others, I seemed to be both looking up at this seat, while at the same time, feeling as if I was in it. It was elusive.

Furthermore, as I observed them bringing these energies down, I knew that I had once come from this place, the *Blue Place and was a delegate to anchor energies and to help keep the portals open between the two places.*

Evidently I lived on Earth, here, but sometimes went *home* to connect with the luminous liquid light and the love energy there because it fed me. I was one of many bringing the light here as a *seed.* I was called the *Queen*, like the bee, and evidently helped generate the colonies here. Now I understand why *I could join the light from above and below during special moments.*

However I was unclear about my occasional visits to my *home planet*. It appeared that this is what my lost heart piece was all about. I kept looking in to receive the real story as it returned to me. Moreover it seemed that I had intended to go back for a visit, but had been stopped.

I had been *captured* and kept here as this *'seed'* because *'They'* wanted me to remain in the Earth. But then I wondered who *'They'* were? Then I was shown a clear vision of how I was wrapped.

I had been entwined like a spool of white thread, made into what looked like a cocoon, in an almond shape and placed into a chamber, a vault, that was kept secret.

Consequently, this "seed piece", my energy, had been *used as a signal to call others.* It felt like my energy was holding the *Divine Feminine* and, in a chamber close by, was another sacred object, one that held the energy of the *Divine Masculine*. I wondered what that could be?

I was informed that together they created balance for the Earth here, the masculine and feminine or the five pointed and six pointed stars, a geometric pattern. *Hummmm,* now I was having some insight about the ceremonies I had been shown to do.

Finally after identifying my tightly wrapped heart piece, the *seedpod,* it seemed to take hours of unwrapping, traversing dimensions before I could place it back in my heart. During the procedure, I suffered excruciating heart pain; the energy seemed too strong. *Ouch! It felt like I had been crucified for thousands of years and only now was I being resurrected.*

My heart's *soul essence* after millennia was justly returned. It brought me a new sense of warmth as I welcomed it back. I asked to receive a gift it might have brought me. It was *Peace.*

Several days passed before I asked a friend to guide me in a past life regression so I could see my *wrapped soul piece* from another perspective. She agreed so we began. After closing my eyes, she led me down steps to arrive at the door of a marble temple. I opened it and moved down to a short doorway at the end of a hallway. I stepped inside to find my past lifetime playing out. I watched.

Again, I started sobbing and couldn't stop. It was deep, deep sobbing. Pain and intense sadness got stuck in my throat, my fifth chakra, so I felt blocked, crying out for relief. Again I watched myself being wrapped up and left in the temple here, stuck, so I couldn't go back up to my other home, the other planet.

Seeing that I needed help in the middle of this regression, my friend interceded, asking, "Do you need permission to speak something or release it out loud?" I heard her words and immediately responded, "Yes!" So I screamed out as loud as I could, declaring,

"MY SOUL ESSENCE HAS BEEN PLACED HERE UNWILLINGLY FOR TOO LONG, SILENCED. NO ONE COULD HEAR ME THEN

BECAUSE I WAS NOT ABLE TO SPEAK ABOUT IT...BUT NOW I CAN!!"

Then I was done, finally. After thousands and thousands of years my emotions were at rest. Then I heard these words:

The Feminine Essence has been held within the Earth for thousands of years and now must come to the surface and be seen! It feels like all women carry this blueprint: of being lost, hidden, unwanted for their truth and of having to assume another identity most of the time. Now however, we are being called back.

Evidently I'd played a big part in this early temple in Rennes Les Bains. After learning about the Priestess Ceremonies we performed to align the Earth with other planetary places, to keep the doorways open, my soul piece felt validated, honored.

Chapter 29 – The Inner Temple

Ever since my feet first touched ground in the Rennes Le Chateau area of France in 1996, drawings and information have come to me non-stop about some Inner Temple there. Consequently, I have guarded this information and my drawings carefully until the time was right to release it. *That time is Now.*

Each experience was built upon the one before, expanding on it. Even if I was sitting peacefully somewhere in the exquisite landscape, my visions wouldn't stop. Something else was always being shown to me.

The ones of which I speak are located in the pentagram, a five pointed star that I call a *Venus Temple*, first written about by Henry Lincoln in his book, *The Holy Place*. He says:

What our ancestors found here was enormously significant to them; their gods had given them a Sacred Place and so they built a stupendous Temple to enclose it, invisible simply because it is too vast to be seen. A gigantic pentagon some 15 miles in circumference, it is laid out on the ground for those with eyes to see, for 'the initiated.'[7]

Certain places I have watched carefully for years, receiving timeless information from the *Guardians* and *Priestesses* there, speaking about what they once did and how it is playing out today, what they want us to know for the future. Moreover I realized all the information and drawings I'd received already have never been recorded in any book about the area. Thus it urged me to trust my visions and the words of these unseen ancestors to pass on the information I speak about now.

In fact, just after moving to Rennes Les Bains, I had a vivid experience at *La Source Sale* related to this "temple." First introduced to me by my friend Rose, I wanted to return and explore it again, especially when a local researcher friend mentioned that a clear green stone was found inside a rock cavern above La Source Sale. He said people had been going there for years, sitting around it in tall rock-like chairs where they had amazing experiences, other dimensional. I wondered if the place he spoke of was located in one of those tall rock structures I noticed at the edge of the field on my first visit there.

Instead of driving up the winding road Rose took me by car, I left my car at the bottom and walked up, to engage myself more directly with the earth energy. It was a solitary pilgrimage, I was told, because there was something important for me to see and learn here.

I crossed the stream as it flowed down from the saltwater source above and as I got closer, I sensed what felt like a pulse coming from the ground. Arriving a short distance from *La Source Sale*, I decided to hide myself in a small cluster of trees, where I stood patiently, watching it.

Shortly after, something came into my awareness. A symbol. First, it was one symbol and then there were two of them; they were identical, curved, like thick bent lines facing each other. They resembled two hands, or two commas, whereby the end of one stopped in the middle of the other, never touching it. I realized that I was seeing the symbols from a top view, a different dynamic than if I were seeing them from the side.

Moving to find a position to observe them from the side, I finally locked into it and saw a spiral come down from the heavens that met another spiral coming up from the Earth. They engaged spatially, intertwining but without ever touching each other. It was fascinating.

Then I went back to view it again from above and glanced in the center of it where the spirals had formed their coma-like design. This time however I discerned it to be an "eye" in the center and soon heard:

I am the EYE, the chip of all being, with the essence of other races and places. It has been planted deep here and has been found but never understood. This is the 'Code of Being'.

Unmistakably, I felt a pulsing that seemed to affect my outer body, causing me to twitch a few times, as the informative voice continued:

We are the Giants, the guardians, protecting this knowledge. We are calling for the 'tribes' to come so we can decode it together. We are gathered in our seats of wisdom around this ancient stone. It is a coded device calling the ancestors. It is a time capsule for years to come that can elevate all beings (who are ready) to the place of the highest consciousness, the other Earth, to evolve into other dimensions. This Earth experience is about that. You are with us already; bring the others.

I was mesmerized both by what they said and what was shown to me, realizing that it was far beyond anything I could have ever imagined. And I knew that this was probably the place my friend had mentioned, where people came to sit around a green stone in their rock-like chairs. But I knew my experience of it was from a different perspective.

Thus, after seeing what I had and feeling slightly

altered, I was ready to descend back to my car. Just as I had finished walking through the last field, I had a sense that I was walking amongst pyramids. They were all lined up beside me, as if each planet and star system were represented. Then the scene appeared to change as I saw ships fly over the area, like UFO-type objects, the likes of which I'd never seen before. Naturally I questioned if I'd just stepped through some kind of timeline or dimensional shift.

Going slowly, I followed the dirt road back to my car, unlocked it, anxious to drive back to Rennes Les Bains. Mistakenly I thought my visions were over, but something seemed to have accompanied me and was moving alongside my car as I drove back. An object of some sort, it glided just above the salt water, which was flowing down through the Fountain Des Amours, then to where it met the other river, La Blanque and flowed into it. Together these rivers became La Sals River.

At this joining place where the salt and fresh waters met, I was aware that this object quickly descended into the Earth, where it seemed to rest like it was in a parking place. Not wanting to look but stretching my vision regardless, I soon saw Beings get out who appeared to be within a funnel of energy. It was like they were coming from the place where the two worlds, the spirals, had engaged. Then I heard:

This is the place where the underground temple begins. Something important is kept inside this temple.

Slipping into my other vision I could see something encased in a glass-like box that was vibrating at such a high frequency that it appeared almost invisible. Then I saw robed women surrounding it as the shimmering energy radiated out at such a high frequency that they too became almost invisible. It was all I was shown as the vision ended.

I was able to step back into the physical world, where I was more comfortable and drove back to my apartment.

Another time, one late July evening after I had moved here, when the summer light had pushed the night away until 10:30 or 11 pm the way it does in France, I was walking along the Sals River with a friend. Suddenly we began noticing that the energy around us had become much stronger, as if someone had plugged in an amplifier that was pulsing high frequencies all around us.

Slowing down, we stopped in a place where young people like to swim in the river when it gets too hot. Our walkway was under a "blue" bridge, another small bridge that connects Rennes Les Bains' main street to the other side, where a restaurant and hotel sit above the hot baths.

To the right of this restaurant, I noticed an old stone archway by itself, once a part of the early Roman bath system here, but which now seemed to lead nowhere. Because it seemed to be an invitation to explore where it now led, we sat down on the pavement where layers of an underground rock ledge were visible in front of us. Closing my eyes, I looked in with my other vision to see what I could.

Quickly a wooden door appeared before me, square with rounded edges. There was a big X on it, with a tall sword placed next to it. I entered. Beings in white robes were gathered around a table as if it were a special meeting place.

Curiously, ever since my first night in Rennes Les Bains, May 1996, when I first arrived to stay at the Hotel de France, a Being in a white robe appeared to me from out of an arched doorway. I had been looking for that doorway ever since. It felt like I just found it.

Entering, I immediately heard a voice tell me, *the inner room is only for 'the initiated',* but I knew they were the ones who followed me on the plane and who helped me find and then claim my lost soul piece. From this moment I sporadically stopped to look in at their council table, to see what they were doing.

Curiously, the next morning I awoke early and began receiving more details of an Inner Temple, encouraged to draw and write down everything I was shown. Details were being given to me from different perspectives of places. Many came from places close to the Little Cascade located all along the river up to where the two rivers crossed at La Blanque and La Sals and slightly beyond it to the place called, La Source de la Madelein.

One early vision of the Inner Temple I experienced was at La Source de la Madelein. Close by the water dripping from the sacred spring there, I was shown long corridors connected to ancient tunnels that came all the way from Egypt. They had originated from under the pyramids. Evidently they had been extended over here through some ancient Egyptian-Atlantis gateway, which I thought intriguing and wondered what they might have brought here.

Then I was shown that the Little Cascade is one of the four entrances into this Inner Temple, one from each direction. Continuing to look in, still seeing with my other vision, I was shown guards standing by each of these entrances at the end of long corridors carved out between high earthen banks on each side. They were wearing the silver colored wire-mesh uniforms that had identified the Knights Templar in the 12th century. It felt like these figures had been standing there since then in some timeless state.

Fascinated as to what they would be guarding so carefully, I was then taken through a passageway down a spiral staircase where I was then in front of an entrance area to some kind of Temple. I could identify paneled walls of a reddish-brown color covered with reliefs along this staircase. Not only were they of round discs, a sun, a moon and a crescent shape, but reliefs of figures appearing to be Priestesses on one side and Priest figures on the other.

At the bottom, looking inside the entrance door, I was shown low corridors going off in several directions to other doorways. Each doorway opened to a different colored chamber. On my left at the end of a low passageway was a red chamber, while a different corridor directly across from me, was a blue chamber. Sloping down under the stairway and close to a place holding water was a passageway leading to a purple colored chamber. Then, in a more isolated area on my right in a green chamber, was, I felt where something ancient might have been hidden.

Lastly, I was informed that these colored chambers translated into different frequency vibrations and that each color chamber worked with levels of consciousness. It reminded me of working around lasers back in my holography days.

I made holograms using a red laser with helium-neon gas, because it was easier to be around for longer periods. It had a lower vibration with longer wavelengths. But the green laser with its argon gas was a higher frequency and had shorter wavelengths. Being around it meant I had to prepare myself, because the energy felt disorienting, intense and I couldn't do it for long.

Then I was instructed to step back, much farther back to where I found the platform leading to another circular stairway down, another place inside this curious inner temple. Although it was still a vision, I felt a smoothness that was comfortable, almost familiar walking down. But then my heart started beating faster. Powerful energies were beginning to affect me so I slowed down. Soon, I could barely move.

There was an enormous circular design on the floor at the bottom, in front of where I was standing. Lines passed through it. Mysteriously, I saw that something was sunken in the center, some kind of a *Box.* I was carefully informed that it contained *The Key,* but I wasn't told to what.

Suddenly I could feel the sensation of wheels here, circles moving; it felt like I had become part of what was being shown to me, no longer just watching.

Then I was aware of other women, Priestesses coming in behind me. We were all gathered in two circles ready to move around this *Box,* slowly. The energy got stronger inside *The Box.* Our bodies became synchronized, moving in alignment together, evidently turning in accordance to some kind of planetary alignment. Suddenly, we stopped. I heard it was because the *point of alignment* was exact. It was the 'axis point'.

Zowie, I shouted to myself from a place deep within. *This is Unbelievable!* It's like some kind of futuristic movie. First I saw *the Box* open and shoot out

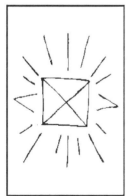

a great beam of gold light. When it arrived at the temple ceiling the ceiling opened too, wide. Then this great beam of light shot far up into the heavens and went directly to Venus, Earth's sister planet.

Magically, as soon as Earth and Venus had been aligned, I saw a gold light be sent back to Earth from Venus. This was a new experience for me. I'd never seen anything like it, vision or other. Then I witnessed all the women, Priestesses, run over to this "returning light" carrying small jars in which to collect it.

Called *Turning the Wheels of Time,* evidently this ceremony has been done since time immemorial, by engaging women to play their part with the universe. It was called *The Way of Oneness.* Furthermore, this special circular chamber was where the *places between the worlds* whose doors only Priestesses could open were known. They were the ones who connected the portals.

Highly trained to hold the vibrations of love in their hearts, if one Priestess was not in this high vibration, if her field was not in alignment with the *circuit of love,* then the portals could not be opened.

Therefore, in order to keep their energies synchronized, there was a place of water access so they could immerse themselves. Certain times of the month they attuned their vibrations here. It re-initiated them and realigned their DNA to the original *blueprint of Divine Cosmic Consciousness,* transforming them together, on a cellular level.

Moreover, if a Priestess was slipping into the Earth energy vibration past being able to carry this light for the inner *work,* there were other jobs for her to do in the Temple. Sometimes it was working with younger Priestesses, otherwise she might go into lifetimes as a *lost soul* having to experience all the lower vibrations to hopefully one day return.

Curiously I learned that this immersion place also made it easier for beings coming in from other constellations or planets who needed to attune and acclimate to the Earth energies, depending on their mission. Some were immersed in the special waters of Rennes Les Bains aided by the Priestesses who augmented the *Fitting Into The Body* ceremonies. It helped them *Carry the Light.* There was a way of using the waters, as a way to *Birth* them, almost as if they

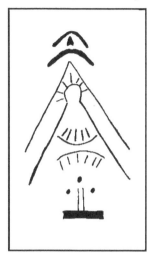

were being *Anointed* or *Baptized* to be able to live on the Earth.

Passed down through the most sacred Feminine Lineages, the knowledge of *ancient water rituals* came from a time when Priestesses were called the *Adjusters of the Waters.*

Then I was shown more about the timeless

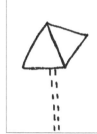

process of coming and going through these portals, evidently used by star beings from elsewhere. It was about coming in, adjusting, being toned, activated and then given the *code of life ethics* here, which included *what they needed to learn.* I was told that:

This is an ancient process of life that has been experimented with on many other planets in the universe. Some chambers were specifically aligned to different constellations and the shapes of them either helped some to return back to their place of origin or to stay here to do some kind of 'work'.

Curious as to what their "work" was, another afternoon while I was walking along the River Sals, I stopped to sit on the bench across from my apartment.

Something urged me to turn and face Pech Cardou, the mountain high above the Little Cascade, when I began to hear words saying: *We are calling you,* so I got out my pen and pad to write.

Since time immemorial this has been a place of 'reading'. Here we come to read and know the records, the laws, the ways of ancient times and the ways of the future. This is where those come who have forgotten. That is why you and the others are here searching for your truth, the Truth.

We are the guardians of this treasure shown to you your first night here. Now it is spiraling out as the world awakens, ready to hear this truth, this knowledge. These 'records' are ready to be seen, known, lived. This is where many came forth in this life to evolve back to Source. This was an experiment that from these waters made it possible.

Then, hesitating he gave me one last detail:

Isis knew how to bring her energy here from her celestial heavens and has always lived in two places. Isis was the first real 'hologram' on Earth the only true 'As Above So Below'.

Wow, I'd never heard Isis called a hologram! This got my attention! Anomalies were part of this great Temple where I was always seeing something new, different, but I had never thought of Isis as a *hologram*.

Time passed, when after facilitating one of my groups and I was back in Rennes Les Bains, I took a walk to my favorite place, the Little Cascade. Sitting across from the pond on a flat, square-ish rock where I often sat, something began moving around in front of me although nothing appeared.

Discerning what it might be, I slowly began sensing that there were lights moving around and watched them dancing on the pond. Then I heard these words:

This is the place of the 'Holy Lights'. If you stand in the middle you can go anywhere if you know where you want to go. The 'direct line' from here goes to Venus, Earth's sister planet. Lifting up to Venus can be fast and easy, if you have no fear.

Then she added:

If we can remember the secrets that are hidden and preserved here we can travel anywhere, know anything, feel and be anything, anyone, through the experience of 'time travel.'

Long ago other forces tried to block this energy so they could control the planet. It was at this moment the 'Arc' - once located here - was put into 'another dimension' for safety purposes. Only those who knew, who were 'initiated' and who had 'heart', the key to the higher vibration, could open it. This is why certain ones are being called now to anchor again the energies and to keep the portals open.

Confused by the proposition of *time traveling* or imagining it, I walked the road home carefully, trying to figure out why I was being shown something like this. As if I was being called to board *a flight,* but not one to some favorite European city or secret island, it was to another *planet,* a place seemingly lost in time, perhaps in the future.

Who would teach me how to step through this ancient doorway *up?* What would I do when I got there? What language did they speak and where would I stay? Could I ever get home? Do people really do this? Maybe I could travel inside one of those tiny diamond pyramids.

I have always watched beings, coming and going here, with my other vision, but I never thought about being one of them in this lifetime. Maybe in other lifetimes, I knew these details. But not now! Confused, I continued my walk home.

Several days later, back for another episode, I had intended to sit by the Little Cascade when mysteriously, something guided me to proceed further up the path to a place I'd been just a few times. I followed the old Roman road higher, sparsely layered with rocks, to where it took a slow turn to the left, where I found what resembled an amphitheatre.

It was an overhanging rock ledge area in a semi-circular shape at the curve of the path on my right, opposite and above the sharp angle the River Sals made on its way downstream. I walked over to stand at the bend and noticed how the river was like a snake on its own mysterious adventure. Then I turned around to face the charming rock amphitheatre.

Without a minute to myself to ponder the mystery of my own life, I quickly became ears to a very urgent message:

This is the place where the Earth 'stands still', where the wheels of time play and turn. It is a place we call the 'eye of the needle', where some can pass while others are not allowed. It is the place of 'sifting' the energies, the reading of vibrations.

This is the place of honoring the Ancestors and the lineages of those who came before, of the Priestesses. Records of who made it to this place are stored and their 'codes' have been left here. It was so they could 'remember'.

We speak of the 'new axis' points when the new lineages will return: of the Pleiades, Sirius, Andromeda, Lyra, Arcturus and many others. They will be returning to participate in the One Mind, One Heart, One Universe.

And this knowledge has been stored in these Ancient Rocks that foretell of this time, for it to be known. The Golden Arc brought here by the Templars was energized here, and is part of a portal of Golden Light now opening to anchor the Feminine Wisdom from other places…. the Truth Star. It holds the origins of us All. It is a place of beginning again.

Those who have 'guarded' them will open the Temple doorways and ready the planet for 'The Light' to return. It is not only for individuals, but All Beings, All Humanity – merging together all races of man – from this planet and elsewhere. This is the true Oneness.

Overwhelmed by the impact of this message, humbled that this resident being had spoken such important words to me, I gave thanks. Standing up, I moved over closer to the amphitheatre, to the middle of this stage-like rock platform to the only spot the sun's rays were shining out from between the distant tree branches.

Here I put my face. As I felt its soft embrace on my cheeks it was as if this light had been shining here since the beginning of time, in this spot, carrying the wisdom of remembrance to all who had forgotten. I was one of them.

Chapter 30 - The Dream

Darkness surrounded me as I woke clutching my chest; the pain was unbearable. Someone was putting a sword into the back of my heart. It was the middle of the night and I was in my apartment bed in the small village of Rennes Les Bains.

Lost in my dream, I saw myself standing against a steep earthen wall wearing a mesh-like garment from head to toe, outside a half-hidden doorway deep within the earth. I was guarding something of importance.

Protected by his sword, a man dressed in a short tunic over his mesh-like body suit had moved hastily down the dark camouflaged passageway that led to where I was. He demanded to know what I was guarding, what was hidden inside. I stood there lit by a thin ray of light that had escaped through a crack in the rocks high above me. Remaining silent, I didn't reply, as if my presence were in some other world far away.

I was a Knight Templar, one of those famous warrior monks from the 12th and 13th centuries in France who went to the Holy Land to supposedly protect pilgrims on the Crusade routes, but whose true mission was to dig beneath Solomon's Temple and find important treasures hidden there. When found, they were secretly brought back into France and stored in special places. This was possibly one of them.

In this dream I remembered having taken an *Oath of Obedience* to a Templar superior, which required having a specific "etiquette" in my routines. Later I was sworn into a *Code of Silence* when I was chosen to guard this doorway, "that I would never tell anyone what I knew."

The elusiveness of this dream made me feel like I had been guarding this treasure for centuries, through a timelessness that asked for my silence in any reality with whomever I met. It felt like there was a legacy attached to the knowledge that could kill me if I broke this silence, as if someone or something was always behind me watching. Maybe it appeared that I was asleep in some realities, resting on the job, but I was awake and would be until it was time for the treasure to be revealed.

The man who had arrived before me was wearing a similar mesh-like garment under his belted short tunic. His sword scabbard was marked with the same Templar insignia as mine when he suddenly appeared.

Then louder, more emphatically he asked me again, "What are you guarding here?" lifting his left arm to point at the door next to me. Again, I gave no reply and turned my back to him. In this moment, like in a flash of lightning, he drew his sword and with authority, thrust it impeccably into the back of my heart.

He didn't know what had been entrusted to me, though assumed I would tell him if he too, were a Templar. I felt his arrogance while falling to the ground, clutching my heart. It was clear he was in disguise, pretending in Templar clothing. With no answer from me he would try to open the door himself.

Fully awake now I sat up in the darkness and tried to pull the sword out of my heart to give myself any immediate relief, regardless of what reality I was in.

The next morning I experienced a painful cough in my chest that would continue to wake me up for months, coughing and coughing, spitting up mucus. Mysteriously it was always at the same time each night. Finally I asked for help.

Chapter 31 – An Invitation

Mystery and intrigue have long been associated with the ancient Order of Knights Templar. After my shattering dream of a man in a wire-mesh garment guarding something as someone thrust a sword through the back of his heart, it got my attention. I wanted to investigate.

Not just anywhere, it happened in the Languedoc area of southern France, more precisely Rennes Les Bains where I was now living. Exploring fortresses, chateaux and "commanderies" in the region once affiliated with the Knights Templar, I was looking for clues. Furthermore I began including some of these places in my itineraries, bringing my groups to experience where they had left their elusive legacies more than 800 years ago.

Interestingly, I befriended a special couple living in Rennes Le Chateau, both Knights Templar and members of a worldwide order in which he was the "commander" of the Languedoc region. Because he was a long time researcher of Templar histories and mysterious treasures, I began inviting him to speak for my groups.

Their home, located between the ancient "Merovingian" Castle in Rennes Le Chateau and the Magdalene church, was once probably a stable for horses used by the last royal family living in this Castle. Made into a small two-story home, it carries an ancient essence, quaint but sacred, with a sword hung on the wall, visible as soon as you step inside.

They extended their hospitality to us and always invited my groups into their garden, that went over to a stone wall at the edge of the steep Rennes Le Chateau hill. Here they had formed a circle of short standing stones.

During one of my groups, a Priestess group, in September of 2006 (when Nicole Christine was co-facilitating with me), and after Joseph had made a wonderful presentation for us, we walked over to create a circle together inside these short standing stones. As we joined our hands, I was about to call in energies to begin a brief ceremony, when my mouth fell wide open.

I heard a swooshing sound and then watched a very tall female figure glide over to join us, ethereally, who was swooshing her sword back and forth with wide moves as she walked across the lawn. *It was her*!

It was the first time I'd seen her since that cold Beltane eve at midnight when she first appeared to me in 1998. Now I was curious to know what she came to do.

Wondering where she'd been for almost eight years, I watched her walk over and stand just outside the circle, the side closest to the house. Then with a wide move she swung her long sword around, lifting it with both hands before she dramatically thrust it into the center of the circle, our circle, into the ground.

I questioned who else was aware of her presence as I watched every color of the spectrum spiral out from this center and touch the heart of each woman. Unmistakably I felt how it uplifted my heart, hoping it did the same for the others. In fact what she did felt truly to be our ceremony. Then I spoke grateful words to her before we continued to do ours.

Curiously, she then began showing herself for a few more of my groups in this same garden, although I was usually the only one who saw her. It was from these moments that I began calling her *Lady Venus*.

Moreover our Rennes Le Chateau experience became the favorite memory of every group I brought there. They always declared that being with Joseph and Frederica always brought warmth and laughter to what might possibly be an intense pilgrimage. Certainly after exploring vestiges of long gone times, such as of the Templars, Cathars and the Holy family here, they brought light into what could for many have been disorientation, if they had uncovered personal memories of past life histories here.

One afternoon while I was visiting them the beginning of my second year living in Rennes Les Bains, we were sitting in their garden talking, when I got up to go pet one of the many stray cats they were feeding. Joseph got up and walked over to me.

Of a medium height with fine brown hair he spoke to me in his slight German accent, "I want to invite you to join the Knights Templar Order, my 'commanderie' to be part of what we do in the world. I have known you for some time now and understand your work, what you offer people."

He stopped and I took a quiet breath before he continued, "I have also invited your friends from the US." Honored by his invitation, I replied, "Yes, I would love to be part of your Order." Because I was living in France, he stated, I didn't have to go through the US Priory of the international Templar Order; I would be part of the French Templar Priory.

Reflecting on it later, I knew it would be a different kind of dedication than my Priestess work. It would be opening another door to something else that was calling me and maybe resurrect some old memories from my past. However the Order is in a different timeline now, with other obligations I realized.

Curious, I looked into this worldwide order, the OSMTH of almost 45 member nations. It stands for *The Sovereign Military Order of the Temple of Jerusalem* and the name went back to the time when their first home was in the Holy City of Jerusalem in the 12th century, then considered the *Cradle of Christianity*.

When I searched to find out more about the Knights Templar beliefs, what I would be stepping into, I found that at its core across centuries, it has been about affirming the "Presence of the Eternal Divine." And their "Code" has always been about the promotion of chivalric ideals of honor and support for their fellow man; it was their goal to have a peaceful co-existence between all nations.

Today, most Knights Templar as in the 12th and 13th centuries can be identified wearing a white mantle with a Red Cross on it. And each carries a sword or has one in his or her possession. I would be required to own one of these mantles marked with the red cross and it would also be customary for me to have a sword. *But I would never be allowed on an airplane carrying a sword, I said to myself*

Consequently, I knew *my sword* would be one of Light, invisible to the physical world but it would always be with me.

I learned, in fact that the Templars honored the sword as a symbol of *light cutting through darkness*; it was a symbol of *initiation, of clear consciousness.* Hopefully my walk would embody this, if it hadn't begun to already.

Lastly I learned that when a Templar wore the white mantle it symbolized that he was protected and would in turn protect others. The red cross on it known as the "Croix Pattee," was known as the cross of universal knowledge. I was touched by this legacy of symbols, high wisdom, wondering if I would feel differently while wearing my own white mantle.

Much has been written and many speculations made about the Knights Templar concerning their true mission. But it may never have been known except by a few, those of the inner circle. After their grand master Jacques de Molay was arrested in 1307 and burned at the stake in Paris by the French King, supported by the Vatican, the order was supposedly disbanded.

Whether the initiations continued is a mystery, although there seems to be documentation that de Molay did transfer his position and title to another before he was burned, when the Order went underground.

Moreover in the early 1800s the Knights Templar Order surfaced again into public view and there are many different orders now, including the Freemasons whose initiations may well have integrated some from the Templars. Some Orders claim to be part of an unceasing lineage that goes back to them.

I also learned that possibly Templar documents and treasure were secretly taken to Scotland and possibly hidden in a place called Rosslyn Chapel, built in the early 1400s by the St. Clair family.

Concerning these treasures, I remember reading that when the first nine knights went to the Holy Land in the 12th century, they secretly dug for something hidden under the Temple of Solomon. Evidently they returned to France where it was said they brought these treasures, placing them somewhere that would be well guarded. But it is still a mystery.

After I received my invitation to join this order I could choose my place of being knighted. Of the many countries represented in the Order and the significant number of Templar priories around the world, there were many possibilities. Interestingly I, and my three

American friends chose Rosslyn Chapel during the fall equinox of 2007. But it would be after I had completed certain required levels of initiation with Joseph, which I did.

Getting ready for my knighting ceremony, I had a white 'mantle' made with the red cross by someone Frederica knew, bought a dark suit, put my Templar insignia on it and found some white gloves. Then I found the proper evening attire for dinner after my investiture, when everyone would celebrate together.

When the time finally came to depart for Scotland, Joseph and Fredericka picked me up and we drove to Carcassonne to board our plane. My present day Templar journey was about to begin.

Landing in northern England, we rented a car. Joseph drove to the town of Rosslyn, on the wrong side of course, the way they do in the British Isles, which I vowed never to attempt doing in this lifetime.

It was sunny and warmish when we arrived in the town of Rosslyn, a tiny village. He parked on a small street and we got out. It was my first visit here, as I faced the Rosslyn Hotel and pub where we would meet the other three who were staying here. It felt familiar.

Turning, I then faced in the other direction toward Rosslyn Chapel and imagined myself in another era whereby I was watching people gathered in this same spot, mostly men on horses. I could hear laughter and celebration before I turned back around. I was back standing at the entrance to the Rosslyn Hotel and pub, where I walked behind Fredericka through the old wooden doorway to meet our three friends for a late lunch.

The softness of the wooden oak tables with a scratch here and there was welcoming. The chairs arranged around them were of an equal warm feeling "broken in," with small antique lamps on each table that could illuminate any darkness. Taking the first swallow of my hot tea brought back a feeling as if I'd been drinking wine and eating the Scottish beef and puddings here endless times before.

I felt at home here. The Scottish people, including the waitresses and the bartenders all had that little twist to their English, which made me smile, wishing they would repeat it again, slower so I could actually understand.

We drove over to check into our accommodations nearby and then all gathered to go over the ceremony details. It would be in French, delivered by the Grand Prior of France. We needed to understand, and know what to reply to questions asked of us like, *Oui, Je suis prete, Yes, I am ready.*

However the present day codes encompassed a different picture of life, we did not have to hide anything or protect anything with *codes of silence, codes of obedience.* More importantly the order did not have to fight or physically kill anyone in the name of justice. I was about to join a modern day Knights Templar Order that was still carrying ancient codes of honor and charity into a new time.

We, the new initiates coming for the ceremony, met the day before our Investiture to tour Rosslyn Chapel together. One by one we stepped into the north entrance of the 15th century stone building. I moved to the left to stand against the wall and let the others pass. I wanted to get my first sense of the chapel alone.

My gaze went up to the slightly arched ceiling where I saw small pentagrams and roses carved out in stone. Having never seen anything similar, I recognized how special it felt to be standing beneath it. Not a basilica or even a large church, Rosslyn was a small chapel. Dripping with details carved in stone everywhere, I realized that no one could ever burn or destroy it easily. It was full of more information on the walls and ceilings than I could ever explore in one afternoon, like a history book opened before me that had been encoded with beliefs, timelines and initiations, waiting to be read by *those who were ready.*

Soon I glided down to the altar area and sat in one of the dark wooden pews facing the central part of the Chapel. I wanted to be still, hoping to tap into what these magical mysteries felt like, hoping that I was *one who was ready.*

While sitting here I noticed something stir inside my heart area, something deep, maybe some kind of hidden feeling that wanted to come forth. But I couldn't name it.

Someone was speaking in a quiet voice nearby talking about the Druids who were once here. She said that the altar was dedicated on St. Mathew's feast Day, September 21, 1446 and that it faced northeast which, according to the Druids was a symbol of the "reawakening of one's inner spiritual forces". *Hummmm...*I thought, maybe that was what I was feeling because we were also here on September 21, the equinox, but it was 661 years later, 2007.

Amidst all the others observing and discussing the chapel, I finally stood up and moved over to find some of the well-known stone carvings of the green man. At first glance some were almost scary, hung upside down, while others had wide carved faces with large sunken eyes or sharp pointed teeth seemingly gagged with a rope in their mouths.

Evidently they represented man's journey through life here also with symbols of rebirth and fertility. They were different. But then I noticed beautiful stained glass windows of Angels between some of these green man carvings.

Most fascinating to me were the famous pillars. In fact our Investiture ceremony would take place at the altar of St. Mathew near two of the famous pillars, *The Master* and *Apprentice Pillars*. The third pillar was behind them, the *Journeyman Pillar,* whose symbolic meaning I already knew reached back to Soloman's Temple in the Holy Land.

Close by these pillars, I heard someone say they were built above a crypt in the Lady Chapel. Then the person said that it was once accessible from the stairs at the rear of the chapel, but curiously was sealed shut long ago. Legends claim that it is a subterranean vault that possibly contains the ancient treasures of the Knights Templar, which might include the Holy Grail as well as important ancient scrolls.

Finally, after a long day of exploring the endless details hidden in Rosslyn Chapel, we were ready to sit down and have dinner together. It was relaxing as I prepared myself for what would be happening afterward. I was excited and could feel it inside, ready for this new adventure that was about to take my life in still another direction.

After dinner I, and my three American friends entered a darkly lit room on the second floor of the hotel. Twenty initiates would be gathering together for a "Vigilance" the night before our Knighting Ceremony. Each initiate had one last chance to examine his or her decision to be invested at this time into the Order.

On the right side of the room next to my friend Gloria, I settled into a chair with a comfortable wooden back ready for what was next. Two Templar officials sat with us silently as we examined any final questions or thoughts we might not have asked.

Then passing in front of us individually, several times, one of the officials would inquire, "Are you sure,

Are you ready, Is this the right time?" And then with each question, I went deeper inside to ask myself, *Am I ready? Was I sure about this? Is this the right time?* Coming back with my decision, "Yes, I was ready, this was the right time, I was sure now." Then after more than an hour, the *Vigilance* was complete, each assured his or her forthcoming ceremony was at the perfect moment. Then we went off to have a restful night before our ceremony the following day.

Several times during the night I woke up, anxious. Not sure why, but I realized this ceremony would be different than my Priestess Ordinations. I was about to join an international Order very visible in the outer world. Compared to the Priestess who is still trying to resurrect herself from that suppressed, seemingly hidden place. Of course she too, and that part of me, wants to once again step out and be recognized for who she is, or I am, thus what we bring to the world.

OK, it's time to get up, I said to myself the next morning. I grabbed a piece of fruit and then showered, putting on my new dark suit with the Templar insignia sewed on the pocket. This was my big day.

Driving over, we met the others outside the hotel including an English woman living in France and a long time friend of Fredericka's. Each of us was carrying our white mantle draped over one arm, as we stood watching several Scotsmen playing their bagpipes, wearing plaid kilts. They were lining the pathway to the Rosslyn Chapel door. Ready, we then walked down to the chapel together. It was official, yes, we were in Scotland and this was really happening.

Protocol had the higher ranked Templar officials proceeding down the short walkway first, inside Rosslyn Chapel to their seats. Then we entered and walked down next to the other initiates. We were directed to the right side a few rows in front of St.

Mathew's altar where the Grand Prior stood beside the three other officials, before they opened the ceremony.

Beginning, the Master of Ceremonies spoke words to honor the ancient Order of Knights Templar and those first nine knights who did the groundbreaking work in the Holy Land of building the first symbolic Earth Temple foundation, dedicated to the Templar codes.

Then he acknowledged the Great Spirit that supports all beings, before he honored the inner temple that we each carry within which supports us. He honored the *As Above, So Below*, and then the ceremony officially began.

Twenty initiates were here from around the world, prepared to be *Invested* into this Knights Templar Order. Each had chosen Rossyln Chapel as his or her place of Investiture. It began. I watched four or five others go before me.

When it was my turn, I went slowly up to stand before the Grand Prior of France. Kneeling down before the ceremonial table between us, on which were candles and special objects, my heart fluttered. He asked me several questions, which I answered in French, after which he stepped forward and lifted his mighty sword above me.

No mistaking, I felt strong grids of different timelines and patterns converging together above me when suddenly I felt another being standing with him. It was a tall female figure. Mysteriously, my other vision showed me how she merged her hand with his and they lifted the sword together.

First he/she reached behind my head, to my back, cutting all or any cords possibly pulling me into the past. Then he/she brought the sword back and lifted it to my right shoulder and tapped, to my left shoulder and tapped before it came over my head. He/she tapped several times as I slowly felt a warm stream of light come in through the top of my head, almost as if it were a pillar of light that went from high above to deep below into the Earth. Lastly, the light moved directly into my heart.

He declared me a *Knights Templar* and officially welcomed me with his final tap, into the Order. Another Templar came from behind carrying my new mantle and put it around my shoulders, joining the clasps together. I was now wearing my white mantle with *La Croix Pattee* on it. As soon as my official ceremonial moment was over, I turned around and walked back to my seat. I was wearing a big smile, like a Cheshire cat.

After each initiate had been touched by the almighty sword and welcomed into the Knights Templar Order as a new member, we stood and sang the Templar motto together:

Non Nobis Domine
It is not in my name oh Lord
Non Nobis
No it is not in my name
Sed Nominis Tuo Da Gloriam
But in your name oh Lord, that is the Glory

Then the ceremony was closed. Everyone fell silent. It was as if a new snow had fallen inside and covered Rosslyn Chapel in white. It was the white mantles everyone was wearing, old and new Templars together. Purity, eternal purity etched out not in timeless stone forms, but in human forms ready to move out into the world and be seen.

We rose together as the officials walked down the aisle proceeded by a member who was carrying a traditionally raised sword as part of this final closing ceremony. As they stepped out the door we, the new members, filed out sometimes in twos. Silently I gave thanks to all those who were also present with me this special day at Rosslyn Chapel.

Again and again I would experience this moment, kneeling before the Grand Prior of France with his ceremonial sword raised over my head, as he tapped it. Clearly, I also remembered the tall being standing before me that cold midnight evening in front of the Tour Magdala, sword in hand. I thought she was Mary Magdalene when she too put her long sword to my head and tapped. I could still feel it. She gave me a mission then and I said *Yes* to it and now I had another one.

Emotional, with a subtle taste of salt in my mouth, I walked out the north door of Rosslyn Chapel, dressed as a Knights Templar wearing my white mantle. I also wore a Red Templar cross that was on a black ribbon over my heart, joining it with the hearts of the original Templars in Jerusalem. And yes, I was also carrying my *Sword of Light*.

I thought of my Scottish ancestors, the Douglas clan from my father's side of the family. They too carried the Knights Templar flag and walked beside Robert the Bruce in Scotland long ago.

Chapter 32– Hidden Temple Secrets

Expanded. My heart felt like it was growing bigger and wider, as though I was becoming like the noonday sun at its hottest and brightest time. A day after my return from Scotland, in Rennes Les Bains, it began.

While I strolled casually next to the Sals River, it appeared that I was taking up the entire path because my energy had grown so big. My steps got slower and slower, when finally, I stopped and sat down on a nearby bench. It took days to integrate what was happening to me, since my *Knighting Ceremony,* so I walked all over Rennes Les Bains, hoping to get more grounded before my next group arrived for eleven days.

On one of these walks I went up toward the place where the two rivers crossed, La Blanque and La Sals. Along the way I was inspired to explore a place where I'd always wanted to spend time. No one was there so I slipped over into the small fairy-like place that was set up as a picnic area. A round grassy spot, it was under tall trees that shaded the picnic table while big stones surrounded it. Near the entrance was a big rectangular rock against which I chose to sit and lean my back. I closed my eyes.

Soon I had visitors, the *She Bears*, the beings in the red furry bodies I first met in Glastonbury, as my inner vision took me into a scene where they wanted to engage me. They wanted to lead me through a doorway into the Earth. *OK,* I said to them in my lucid state and followed. Very quickly I found myself in a place lined with trees on each side as their branches arched above the center of the path.

Together we walked until suddenly the trees turned into a gold color, when I realized we'd just passed through a *veil,* an entrance to somewhere else. We kept walking.

Figures wearing white robes began appearing on each side of the path. I gasped, noticing their trance-like sleep, some standing, some bent over in their seats as if a *spell* had been put on them. They were guarding something or waiting for something. We kept walking.

As we moved closer, bright lights, rays were suddenly filtering out from somewhere. We continued. Lastly, I saw a box in the center surrounded by a big square like a pyramid. *Was it the Arc* I asked myself?

With no decisive answers, only questions the scene ended and I was back in my body propped against the rectangular rock on the ground. These white-robed beings seemed more like humans, not some beings from another dimension. In fact these Beings in their trance-like state reminded me of famous drawings I'd seen depicting Templars seemingly collapsed in front of the Holy Grail guarding it or waiting for the spell to end so they could wake up.

After this elusive experience, interestingly, I was ready to facilitate my group arriving the next day; the intensity of my heart had settled.

After the group had departed and I was back in my apartment in Rennes Les Bains, musing on the group experience. I recognized that it was the first group I ever remembered facilitating in which nine women flowed so well together. Everywhere we went, all that we did, felt like we did it with one mind, one heart. It changed me so much so that *I let go inside.* Not sure of what exactly, but I definitely asked myself, *What else is there?*

Joyful, I was ready to step out for a walk, the first since my group left. Again I choose to go in the direction where La Blanque and La Sals Rivers met. On the way I passed over a low short bridge where cars could cross. I decided to sit and dangle my feet in the water. It seemed a good time to release any remaining issues I'd been holding onto in my life, to empty my inner chalice. Facing downstream, I let the waters take them all away.

I included old family beliefs, old partners and even childhood stuff, while also giving thanks to my parents. But as I released early childhood wounds, I noticed some deep emotion and tears coming up.

Too soon however, several cars approached, wanting to cross the bridge; I was obliged to move. Having released my old attachments, giving them to the river to take away, I wasn't able to face the opposite direction with the water flowing toward me to receive new energies and fill my empty chalice. Thus, I decided it would come to me as I continued toward the place of the crossing.

Just before arriving at the crossing, another spot along the river called to me. Curiously, it was diagonally across from the enticing picnic spot where the *She Bears* had led me on a journey where I saw beings lost in some spell.

But this spot was above two waterfalls, one higher and one lower. I walked over to the cooking pit by the side of the road where I'd seen vans often parked overnight. Finding the narrow dirt path behind it, I was led down to a ledge, which I climbed over. Navigating the oddly shaped jutting rocks below it, I carefully maneuvered my feet onto an area of long flat rocks.

As I faced the river coming towards me, I found water streaming out from a few small half-hidden holes under the riverbank. One was shaped like a yoni, as waters flowed out tinged with red. Passing it, I tasted the water to find it full of iron, a similar taste to the waters of the Red Spring at The Chalice Well in Glastonbury.

Dodging between immersed rocks, I found a dry flat rock nearby where I laid down between the low falls on my right and the high ones on my left. I stretched out, soothed by the healing sounds of the waterfalls, questioning why I hadn't come here earlier. Some blocked emotions I'd sensed previously came up, when, after feeling into them to get beyond their hold on me, they dissolved and soon passed, leaving me feeling free and cleared.

But as soon as my inner vision began opening again, something started to happen. Another movie began playing out from far below these waters. Without hesitation I was taken directly in to see it. *What's happening now*, I asked myself? *I see a room with tablets inside.*

Not having to go down spiraling stairs to reach any hidden doorway, I moved quickly into a circular room. *There they were. I could see stone-like tablets standing up in four directions with two more in the center on the ground lying together. Each of the four directions had a Guardian.*

Furthermore, I felt that these tablets were sometimes empty until symbols appeared on them. Quickly I realized *I knew these symbols and could draw them.* No, it wasn't words on these tablets... only symbols. Each was totally different; each direction had a different message. Together *they carried the 'whole' message, the whole experience.*

Interestingly they reminded me of a hologram, when, if broken, each piece carried the entire message, but from a different perspective or point of view. Then I received a strong message that was giving more specific information about these tablets:

These writings are about an ancient place, a place of access to an inner dimension within oneself where all is peaceful and in harmony, in the great forest, where everything is alive. The symbols will take you there, if you are willing and courageous enough to go. This place has been put here so we will remember on this planet – if everything else is gone. The ancient Ancestors created this.

This is the place of peace and safety within, that great 'Emerald Forest' where all things are possible. It is the place of knowing what this world, this life is all about, why we are here. It is a place where there is no death, just pure energy, the spirit of all things, where life begins. This inner landscape gives clarity if one listens to the messages on these 'tablets.' Follow these simple ways and the true life on Earth will be revealed.

Fumbling quickly in my backpack I found my larger pad and started to receive the 6 drawings. Then I received words of guidance that went with each tablet, a message to hear while experiencing them.

As I began to look at the symbols and speak the short writings, I noticed that their energy helped me feel fresh and energized, beyond any sense of being tired. I felt great peace in my heart.

Later at my apartment, I made larger drawings of them and cleared everything else off my walls to put them up. It was my new *Temple*. Then I received a longer more expansive message about these *Tablets,* disclosing that:

These Codes are here now to help humanity. Hundreds of thousands of years ago, the Caretakers or the 'Council of Nine'...the 'Elohim'... decided that in this place and on the Earth, there needed to be knowledge available, stored in a safe place so humanity could find it for reference. This area, this Great Temple, was placed here to be a receiver and to emanate the Divine Christ Light. There are nine other places as such on the planet that hold this energy.

This knowledge was passed down to the Knights Templar to be guardians, but they have forgotten. They did not speak it, but knew it and lived it. It was never written. They were carrying on a lineage that was long ago established on this planet from other places, each offering initiations, wisdom, from where it all began, the thread that unites us all.

We have been coordinators of ceremonies to be remembered here on Earth. These ceremonies help the Earth maintain her connection to her sisters in the heavens. The Earth has many layers and levels of life in her body, but because we cannot see them does not mean they are not here. They are. Many have been here long before those who are visible on Earth have lived.

*Life first began within the Earth with the **Great Race**, those Beings who were known as the **Code Carriers**. They were the ones who gave the Earth her Life, we could say, her Heartbeat, like any birthing process. There were nine Temples that carried the Light Codes and gave substance to the Earth, as every body of matter in the universe has consciousness. And Earth was our choice to watch. **We are the Watchers**.*

These Light Codes marked the places within the Earth where all could come for safety, to remember and to commune with the Ancestors, the Great Race when necessary. One could access this place anytime. They have been waiting for us to make contact, but we have forgotten.

We think they are coming from 'above' but they are already here in the Earth in this special Temple, waiting for us to be ready. Their lives have been harmonious in the Mother Earth because they have found the system, the formula to come and go, back to the Source ever communicating, remembering, being in union with the One Mind, One Heart, One Source.

There are places where time is 'kept', where the wheels turn, where the keepers of the essence of the Earth abide. Every planet has a system, a people, a theology, something that unites them. We are the Council of Nine coming from above and below, from the source of All, overseeing, watching ...remembering.

The Temples of the Earth are in geometrics of power, so nothing can penetrate. Many have visited, experienced and remembered here. There have always been guardians of these places who have taken **Vows of Obedience** *which is why the* **Order of Honor** *was introduced here as the 'Knights Templar,' so they could keep the peace. Then* **Codes of Silence** *were initiated for those who guarded special secrets. It has always been this way, until the 'disruption,' the mismanagement of energies, manipulation, when other beings intervened, they who had forgotten.*

From this moment of inner disharmony, it has affected the outer Earth. Now we have war, mistrust, fear, all because the Love was lost, the trust was lost and our safety was lost. The question has been, 'When am I safe, in what place and whom can I trust? What have I forgotten?'

Once we were a people of such high integrity living in harmony on this planet where our foundations are, were. Once we honored the yearly cycles, when the stars and planets guided our way. We knew the star systems, the constellations, because it was part of us. We felt the influence within the Earth before we saw anything outside, before we experienced the outer world, the physical world, when we lived from our souls.

. The inner Earth is light and peaceful, with mountains, rivers and lakes. The Temples helped balance our hearts, our lives, as their structure harmonized the within and without of the planet. We had different rooms, each with an important function: of blue, green, red, purple and gold light. The rooms were shaped to fit the color and distinct function of the vibration.

We had caretakers of each, ones who guarded and maintained the finite vibrations. They were no ordinary guardians, only those who knew their way, familiar with the nooks and crannies of the Temples and the places where the "un-invited" could hide who tried to take over many times, to steal our treasures. Some survived this 'guardianship', the 'watching' and some did not. It was a big job, a courageous one. You were one of these beings, defending it until the end, which you did, ready to give up your life. These qualities have always been with you.

Tablet Drawings: *East, South, West, North, Middle Two In The Middle.*

These words were given to me to hear or to read as one faces each tablet

Tablet of The East:
Time is waiting... .Be still and Honor Self... Merge, so you will know Love

Tablet of The South:
Access the Light... extend your filaments... Open all doorways within ... Peace comes Forth

Tablet of The West:
Pull your Codes up... Extend them to the Heart... Knowledge is here...

Tablet of The North:
The Ancestors are here... and there... Ask... Receive... Live with (in) them here... Joyful Blessings on Earth...

Peace
Middle Tablets: *Abundance is Love...Love is Abundance*

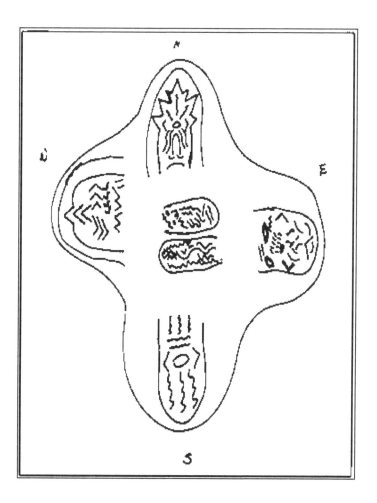

(I plan to make a separate book of these tablets, in which each tablet is drawn separately, so you can take each out to place in your own *Temple*, for a proper transmission.)

Chapter 33 – HER STORY

Lastly and very importantly it is time to hear the *Lady With the Sword* tell her own story. She has been with me since our first meeting, that cold midnight on Beltane eve in front of the Tour Magdala in 1998.

I began my *mission* in France as a Priestess searching for ancient wisdom I thought Mary Magdalene brought here. I wanted to make it available for others. But later I realized this wisdom never left; it has been here since the beginning.

Often it was a Priestess speaking to me, as if she and I were one. But it was the one with the sword who would have the ultimate word. She would summarize not only my quest, but that of all Priestesses who come to understand the mysteries of the Rennes le Chateau area. But first she wishes to speak:

You want to know "my story" but truly it is your story. You have been called to tell others the truth about when we were One. We are the Priestesses who came here to this planet to anchor the energy of Love, to make this a planet of beauty and Oneness for all to know.

We came from another place, sent by the great one who carries her "Sword." She is the one who cuts through all that matters not, to get to the only thing that does matter – the connection between the above and below. We the Priestesses are the anchors of light, setting the 'codes' in the Temples and laying the foundation for those who will follow.

We mark and watch the movement of the heavens and record it on Earth, knowing what energies and ceremonies are appropriate, when certain celestial bodies are aligned with the Earth. We are and have been responsible for all that happens, good or bad. Others have often tried to stop our ways, wanting to control what we have always known.

We each have a tiny seed deep within our soul ready to be birthed, ready to open and be seen, revealing all the light we carry. It's who we are and have always been. Each person carries this same seed, the seed of light and love. It's All there is.

We come from Source, the place of all beginnings. We have keepers in places on the planet who have been the guardians of much knowledge. When we arrived on Earth, we accepted that there are many experiences, things we felt and learned that are different from where we came, not as pure or easy from the teachings and lives we have already known.

That day we arrived we set up places of sacredness, Temples and other such places where we could leave messages for ourselves to one day reclaim, when it was time. And it is time. I have claimed mine, now it is your turn to claim yours. Are you ready?

Days later, another message came, when finally the tall being with the sword identified herself:

*I Am Lady Venus and I have come to tell you a story. I Am Lady Venus, **Bringer of Light** and **The Ways**. It is an ancient system that we carried here to bring the wisdom of life to this planet...of coming and going, being and not being, hearing and being silent. It is about keeping the system in balance, life. We bring* *what has been hidden – out – just as the torus moves, turning and turning, in, out, up, down, inside, outside.*

I am here to retrieve what has been lost, played with, to set the cycles back in rhythm and what the early Temples were about. Each chamber had a value, a focus, a vibration. If one came from a planet or galaxy and needed to rebalance their energy to endure the lower vibrations here, it was done. Usually there were three phases necessary before one could walk out in a physical form if that was their purpose.

Those who stepped out had things to complete here. They worked to weave the light they carried into this physical world, affecting all those who had forgotten. It is they who know how to come and go as light beings, descend through the Temple vibrations to be here and then to ascend once again. It was a miraculous procedure aligned with planetary movements. Different doorways were opened in these moments, as if it were a pick-up station.

There are beings in the Earth who came down centuries ago, some millennia, and they have been weaving and anchoring the light and codes here since then. Some walked out on the Earth one day and some are still deep within it. They are a joyful bunch moving slowly as they do their work.

*It is they who have anchored the light here as well as crystals and other devices not yet known to the Earth community. This is the 'core' that carries the Divine Designs. It is this place where so many have tried to enter, wanting to know, '**What is hidden here**'?*

It is an ancient formula of particles… tiny…tiny... that hold the 'structure'. It is the Basis of All Civilizations, All Life. *It comes from here, the Center. Every formula of life or any living thing has a different shape, whatever that may be. It is a geometric and so are you. It is within each and every one of us and it is* *our journey to wake it up, bring it back to life.* **This has been a Secret**

The Magdalene is about this structure, this ancient pattern. *There are many names for this structure but the definitive one is:* **The Holy Grail.**
And this is the true story. *You have found the answer. Keep walking this path there is no end to it. One pattern leads to another...and another...and another...*

Chapter 34 – And Now

*S*tructures… The Magdalene… The Holy Grail… suddenly everything got simplified. *And now what,* I asked myself?

I knew after so many centuries, that finally, I had stepped out of my *Code of Silence.* My long commitment had ended and I was liberated. Realizing that I had been one of the guardians of these ancient tablets for so long, I knew it was now time to reveal them to the world and that truthfully, this was their real beginning.

From the moment I drew the tablet symbols larger just after receiving them, that little voice inside informed me that the time was approaching to step back into the world of holography, so I could render the tablets dimensionally, in 3-D. I would then take them out to the world for all people to experience their message. Now I ask myself, *Am I ready to travel far and wide to take these to others? Well…Yes,* I answered, *but I would invite other people to assist me.*

Then I remembered an evening up at Rennes Le Chateau during a windy concert of harp, violin and beautiful singing, when suddenly I saw a very large chalice rise up from deep within the hill, a vision. It seemed like mysterious arms were lifting it, but it was blocked, covered by a square shaped object as it rose. Quickly that object disappeared and the chalice was open to receive communication from the cosmos. Had the music raised it up? Had the music broken it's spell, blockage? It seemed so.

I also questioned if it was coming up from one of those 'secret places' hidden below Rennes Le Chateau that held the ancient structure on the planet, as Lady Venus mentioned. *Did this chalice represent the mysteries of the Magdalene now being revealed as the Holy Grail*, I questioned? The vision opened my heart, my memory. Possibly it was a symbol for all women who have been searching, to let go and receive long hidden mysteries of who they are. I know France has brought me closer to my feminine self, assisted by words from unseen guides, priestesses, reminding me of so many forgotten truths. Perhaps you, who have been journeying with me, agree.

Again, after receiving Lady Venus' message about the structure of all things, I remembered another vision I had late in the 1980s. While still working in the upstate New York schools teaching holography, I experienced what might have seemed like some far-fetched concept flash into my mind. It informed me that the structure of all disease was a geometric pattern. It felt so true that I wanted to one day make dimensional images of beautiful soothing scenes of nature in which a person could stand daily or weekly. The geometric composition of it would not only include the structure to heal their specific disease, but would make it a more uplifting experience.

From my photography background I knew that all photographs and paintings had a structure within them, a composition that moved a person's eye around the entire image. Each composition is composed of a subtle geometric shape or shapes, be it a circle, a square, triangle or other. When I taught several week-long black and white photography workshops on Martha's Vineyard Island in the early 1980s, at the end of each, I had the participants line up ten of their final prints so we could see the composition each person used. Often it was the same re-occurring geometric pattern.

Later I did an experiment with a well-known painter on the island who did landscapes. I noticed that his compositions were very angular, because he used triangles and squares. I asked if he would make his next painting to incorporate a circle composition and to use a color he rarely used, red. He did. In his next show it was the first painting that sold. Amazed, he continued exploring the different geometries.

Learning the structures of diseases would require research, so when the time was right I would do it. Furthermore, I wondered if maybe three-dimensional images of the tablet symbols might coincide with the healing of diseases? Only time would tell.

Lastly, on a recent visit to the Little Cascade in Rennes Les Bains, while sitting by the lower pond, I looked up at a place I hadn't stood since 1997. Inspired, I walked around to that side, slightly higher and leaned against a narrow tree.

Warm waters were trickling down in front of me from a place above as I turned to face the lower pond. Staring into the ripples the gentle wind was moving toward me, I suddenly noticed a snake lift itself out of the water to face me. Yes, I had slipped into my other vision, my other reality.

The snake remained steadfast before me, but then straightened its body from the curving upward shape into what soon appeared to be one single line displaying codes inside, DNA codes, I was told. Then it morphed into the form of a female figure, a Goddess. Affirming that I had perceived correctly and she was indeed female, she faced me and spoke quickly:

I am connecting the worlds, the above and the below here. The wisdom I carry is being implanted into the waters and these codes inside me are my 'codes of origination.'

Immediately, I realized she was alluding to her having come from another place, like a star system or a planet. This also reminded me of the unbraiding of the DNA I witnessed here in 1997, while I was in this same exact spot. That time two strands came from one, which I drew as accurately as possible, but this time there was only one strand.

Shortly after, I walked back to the other side, searching to see if there were any physical snakes in the water. There were none. As I moved around close to the lower rocks, I found the step-like rocks that took me to the higher pond, opposite where I had just been standing. As I lifted my right leg, I noticed a thin, brownish-yellow snake below. It was real.

Mingling around a tree with intricately woven exposed roots, the snake suddenly noticed my presence. Quickly it retreated inside the roots. When I got to the upper pond, I sat down in full view of them, hoping the snake would come out. Patiently watching, waiting, a small narrow head finally slithered out from its cavernous hideout.

Its subtle brownish color seemed to merge with that of the tree, as it found a safe ledge below the roots. Slowly, almost deliberately it then maneuvered itself into some kind of unusual form, some kind of symbol. Carefully, I reviewed what it appeared to be, a big arch, almost like half a circle, elongated, before I noticed what seemed like turned up feet at each end. Mesmerized, yet slightly in shock, I exclaimed to myself, *It's the Omega symbol. It means 'The End.' I knew there was the Alpha symbol that means 'The Beginning,' but this is the Omega symbol. Was this a message to me my work is complete here?*

I reviewed the thought and realized, *Yes, I knew there was truth to it, for now.* Glancing at the snake, I saw it was still laid out in the same symbol. Quietly, I did a prayer and gave thanks to all those who had been part of my journey at the Little Cascade over the years, part of my adventure. Then I stood up, found the narrow path above me close to the hill, walked slowly over the tiny footbridge and left. I didn't look back.

Footnotes

Chapter 8
1) *Priestess of Avalon, Priestess of the Goddess*, Kathy Jones, Ariadne Publications, Glastonbury, Somerset, England 2006

Chapter 10
2) *Priestess of Avalon, Priestess of the Goddess*, Kathy Jones, Ariadne Publications, Glastonbury, Somerset, England 2006

Chapter 17
3) *The Sacred Prostitute, Eternal Aspect of the Feminine,* Nancy Qualls-Corbett, Inner City Books, Toronto, Canada 1988

Chapter 18
4) Article, *The Ankh*, from *The Master Key to the Mystery System of the Ankh,* Laird Scranton, published August 26, 2010
5) Article, *Sound*, Catherine Ghosh, published first in *Integral Yoga Magazine* in 2008 than later January 23, 2012

Chapter 21
6) *Genisis, The First Book of Revelations,* David Wood, Baton Press, Kent England, 1985

Chapter 29
7) *The Holy Place,* Henry Lincoln, by Jonathan Cape, Gloucestershire, England, 1991, reprint 2005 Arris Publishing Ltd., England

ACKNOWLEDGMENTS

When one takes a journey such as I have, there are people who have impacted my experience to whom I would like to give thanks.

The first is the great Goddess herself who called me to bridge my memory from thousands of years past. She called me to the sacred lands, beginning with Sedona and continued to southern France, the Rennes Le Chateau area, where much of this book is focused.

I am grateful to all my teachers no matter how great or small it seemed their contribution. First, I want to thank Robert Shapiro who gave me a basis from which to understand the many realities that would serve as a foundation for my quest. And other contributors who assisted me with a deeper understanding of myself are: Sandra Cosentino my earliest Sedona friend, Nicole Christine creator of the Priestess Processes, and all my Priestess sisters from Nicole's lineage (and other) who have walked the feminine path alongside me, which also includes Ann Bauden, Christy Salo, Elizabeth Keller and Ani Williams. A thanks to Suzanne McMillan-McTavish founder of Sedona Vortex Tours who gave me a different kind of courage, Kimron Webb for his teachings, George Schmid good friend and supporter, and then Aurora Spuhler, always there to assist. Then I want to thank special shamanic teachers: Sandra Ingerman and then Michael Harner, of the Foundation for Shamanic Studies.

I'd like to thank my France family: Rose Drevard, Toby and Gerda Dobler, dear Ingrid, Rayseen Horan a companion for adventure, Joanna Westerveld, creator of a wonderful B&B my groups loved, Kaj and Sus Lillenthal and to all the women who participated in my

Magdalene group while I lived in France and even after. And I thank Michael Knaak and Indie for their gracious presence.

From the British Isles I am grateful to Kathy Jones for all that she has done to assist the feminine return in Glastonbury, England and then to Lady Olivia Robertson, co-founder of the Fellowship of Isis for all her wisdom and support of women on the path.

A great thank you to Henry Lincoln who first stepped out to present the hidden mysteries of the Magdalene and Jesus enigma (with Michael Baigent and Richard Leigh) in the long story which also involved the Rennes Le Chateau area. I am grateful to Margaret Starbird who helped define more of these lost stories in her books, as well as to the many other writers who shared their research to help us all understand various other aspects of this elusive story.

Finally I give thanks to those who have assisted me to complete the writing and publication of this book: Luminous Antonio for her coaching, Naomi Rose, editing, and cover design, Lane Badger, for ongoing support. I also thank Rama Cogan and Tom Bird for helping me to understand the writing process, and then thank Melissa Bowersock for helping me with the final process to have my book ready.

But there is one more person I would like to thank. It is my father who told me as a teenager, when he recognized that I was different from other young women from New Haven, Connecticut, that: "The world is your oyster and you can do whatever you want." His words stayed with me my entire life and inspired me to follow my heart no matter what path I chose.

About Nancy Safford

Nancy Safford published her first book as a young photojournalist, before pioneering holography (the 3-D image) in New York State schools as an interdisciplinary approach to education through her non-profit research institute. After moving to the southwest she became a shamanic healing practitioner, an ordained Priestess of the Magdalene Mysteries, a ceremonialist and a clairvoyant reader and life coach. Since 1996 Nancy has been facilitating women's circles and guiding people on pilgrimages to sacred sites in southern France, as a bilingual guide and researcher of the legacies and mysteries of Mary Magdalene, the Cathars and Knights Templar. She has been a spiritual guide in Sedona, Arizona and the southwest since that time, dedicated to empowering others to remember their own wisdom, for a more conscious, authentic relationship within themselves and to know their Divine purpose on the planet.

.